A Christian's Rule of Life

with

Darts of Fire

A Christian's Rule of Life

with

Darts of Fire

by
St. Alphonsus Liguori

with Introductions and brief summary notes
by
Charles D. Fraune

2024
Slaying Dragons Press Classics

Copyright © 2024 by Slaying Dragons Press.

ISBN: 9781961721050

All rights reserved. No part of this publication may be reproduced, stored in a retrieval system, or transmitted, in any form or by any means, electronic, mechanical, photocopying, recording, or otherwise, without the prior written permission of the publisher except for the use of brief quotations in a book review or scholarly journal.

A Christian's Rule of Life is from the Ascetical Works, Volume One: *Preparation for Death, or, Considerations on the Eternal Truths*.

Darts of Fire is from the Ascetical Works, Volume Four: *The Incarnation, Birth and Infancy of Jesus Christ; Or, The Mysteries of the Faith*.

Both editions are from the Centenary Edition. Edited by Rev. Eugene Grimm, Priest of the Congregation of the Most Holy Redeemer.

Cover designed by Caroline Green.

Visit *www.SlayingDragonsPress.com* for publications on the topic of spiritual warfare, prayer, and the Christian pursuit of holiness.

www.SlayingDragonsPress.com
2024

Dedicated to St. Alphonsus Liguori

Table of Contents

PREFACE	xiii
The Church's High Esteem for St. Alphonsus Liguori	

A CHRISTIAN'S RULE OF LIFE

INTRODUCTION	1
"A Christian's Rule of Life"	
CHAPTER I	7
THE MEANS OF PRESERVING THE GRACE OF GOD	
§ 1. To Flee From the Occasions of Sin	9
§ 2. Mental Prayer	11
§ 3. The Frequentation of the Sacraments	13
§ 4. To Hear Mass	15
§ 5. The Visit to the Most Holy Sacrament & to the Blessed Virgin	16
§ 6. Prayer	17
CHAPTER II	19
ACTS & PRACTICES OF PIETY	
§ 1. Acts & Different Prayers on Rising in the Morning, & During the Day	21
§ 2. Method of Making Mental Prayer	24
§ 3. Acts to be Made by Way of Preparation & Thanksgiving Both for Confession & Communion	28
§ 4. Method of Hearing Mass	35
§ 5. Acts to be Made in Visiting the Most Holy Sacrament & the Divine Mother	37

§ 6. Christian Acts, to be Made in the Evening Before
   Going to Bed   39
§ 7. Devout Prayers to Jesus & Mary to Obtain the
   Graces Necessary for Salvation   43
Prayers to the Blessed Virgin Mary for Every Day in the
   Week   45

CHAPTER III   53
THE PRACTICE OF THE CHRISTIAN VIRTUES
§ 1. The Practice of Humility   55
§ 2. The Practice of Mortification   59
§ 3. The Practice of Charity Towards our Neighbor   63
§ 4. The Practice of Patience   67
§ 5. The Practice of Conformity to the Will of God   73
§ 6. The Practice of Purity of Intention   77
§ 7. Rules for Avoiding Tepidity   79
§ 8. The Practice of Devotion Towards the Great Mother
   of God   81
§ 9. On the Practice of Certain Means by Which We May
   Acquire the Love of Jesus Christ   83

DARTS OF FIRE

INTRODUCTION   89
   "Darts of Fire"
I   95
II   97
III   99
IV   101
V   103

VI	105
VII	107
VIII	109
IX	111
X	113
XI	115
XII	117
XIII	119
XIV	121
XV	123
XVI	125
XVII	127
XVIII	129
XIX	131
XX	133
XXI	135
XXII	137
XXIII	139
XXIV	141
XXV	143
XXVI	145
XXVII	147
XXVIII	149
XXIX	151
XXX	153
XXXI	155

XXXII	157
XXXIII	159
XXXIV	161
XXXV	163
XXXVI	165
XXXVII	167
XXXVIII	169
Summary A Curated Selection of the Daily Counsel of Saint Alphonsus Liguori	175
Summary A Curated Selection of the Wisdom of Saint Alphonsus Liguori	179
About Slaying Dragons Press	

PREFACE

The Church's High Esteem for St. Alphonsus Liguori

In order to properly convey to the reader the value of the writings of St. Alphonsus Liguori, following the example of the editors of the *Centenary Edition of the Works of St. Alphonsus,* I would like to present many of the statements of approval issued by the Church, in particular by numerous sovereign Pontiffs. The following is a summary of the Preface to the Centenary Edition, which is contained in the first volume of the Ascetical Works, in which the editors presented this inspiring information.

~~~

The writings of St. Alphonsus Liguori were praised both during his life as well as after his death. The learned Pope Benedict XIV, for example, "approved very highly of the writings of the Saint, and in a letter addressed to him in regard to his Moral Theology, expressed the belief that his work would prove most welcome and useful to the whole Christian world." Pope Clement XIV, who had the special favor from Our Lord to be assisted at his death by St.

Alphonsus himself,[1] had held, in his life, "the highest esteem for the Saint." The veneration felt for St. Alphonsus by the sovereign Pontiffs was such that Pope Pius VII desired to "to possess as relics the three fingers of the right hand with which the Saint had written his works and defended the honor of God, of the Blessed Virgin, and of our holy religion."

It was this same Pope who confirmed the judgment of the Sacred Congregation of Rites which, on May 3, 1803, had decreed that the printed and unprinted works of St. Alphonsus Liguori contained "nothing that deserves censure." Twelve years later, in 1815, Pope Pius VII further approved a decree of the same Congregation which highlighted the divine favors which had been bestowed upon St. Alphonsus. It stated that God had called St. Alphonsus "that he should shine by the light of apostolic virtues" as one of the "stars that … shine in the firmament of the Church militant." Through his obedience to God's call and graces, St. Alphonsus, "like the sun that sends its rays everywhere, … sent forth rays of virtues, worthy of an apostle, when he condemned the honors of the world or showed by his voice and his writings, the road of justice to those who were wandering about in the dark night of this world, that they might be able to pass from the power of darkness into the light and the kingdom of God; or when he gave the best rules to his disciples whom he called members of the Congregation of the Most Holy Redeemer; or when, as Bishop, he united fortitude to meekness, and adorned his crown with the ornaments of the other virtues like so many heavenly jewels."

By declaring him a Saint, the Congregation stated that this would be a cause of great joy for the Church. It would be an event in which the faithful would be inspired and reminded that, though the world and the times change, the Church of Christ will never change nor perish, and "that the spirit of

---

[1] This is a wonderful story. St. Alphonsus, the greatest moral Doctor of the Church, also possessed many mystical gifts. Among them was the gift of bilocation in which he was able to be with the dying Pope at the moment of his death. This occurred in the context of an ecstasy when the Saint was at prayer, something he had experienced numerous times before.

The value of the writings of St. Alphonsus is a recurrent theme in the praises issued by the sovereign Pontiffs. In addition to what has already been presented, Pope Pius IX, in writing to the Saint's Order, the Congregation of the Most Holy Redeemer, on November 25, 1846, expressed "his joy and consolation on hearing that the German edition of the works of Saint Alphonsus had met with so great success." The reason for this joy was because it came "at a moment … when by the insidious devices of the enemies of religion so many pestilential books are in circulation on every side, to corrupt and deprave the minds and morals especially of those not on their guard against them."[4]

Reading his writings, this Holy Father added, "cannot but be of the greatest advantage, not only to Christians in general, but also to ecclesiastics, and to those especially who have the care and the direction of souls. For the works of that most holy and most learned man, written with an extraordinary tenderness of piety and devotion, breathe in every page a special love for Jesus Christ, and confidence in His merits and mercy; they inspire the highest devotion to the Virgin Mother of God and to the saints; they inflame men's hearts with the desire of frequenting the most holy Sacraments, and furnish a most copious supply of excellent admonitions, counsels, and injunctions for procuring and carrying on the work of the salvation of souls."

After hearing these rich praises of his holy writings, it is not surprising that it was this same Pope, Pius IX, "who graciously responded to the petition of many Cardinals, Patriarchs, Archbishops, Bishops, and other dignitaries"[5] and

---

clergy to adhere to the practice of Saint Alphonsus, in order that uniformity might be attained."

[4] This is another reason why the effort of bringing forth the writings of this great Saint are needed in our generation.

[5] The decree established him as a Doctor of the Church added: "Very many cardinals of the Holy Roman Church, almost all the prelates of the whole Catholic universe, the generals of religious orders, the theological faculties of the most celebrated universities, illustrious chapters of canons and learned men of every ecclesiastical body, have presented petitions to our Holy Father Pius IX, Supreme Pontiff, in which they express their common desires that Saint

declared Saint Alphonsus to be a Doctor of the Church. Even more striking is the fact that, at that time, the Church had not bestowed this distinction on any ecclesiastical writer or theologian from the previous five centuries.[6]

Within the decree which placed him among the Doctors of the Church, we find further examples of the Church's high regard for St. Alphonsus Liguori:

> Among those who have done and taught, and whom our Lord Jesus Christ has declared should be great in the kingdom of heaven, is rightly counted Saint Alphonsus Maria di Liguori, Founder of the Congregation of the Most Holy Redeemer, and Bishop of Saint Agatha of the Goths. He shone as a watch-light on its tower, giving examples of all virtues to those who follow Christ and are of the household of God. Already, because of the brightness of his light, he has been reckoned among the Saints, the domestics of God. But what he reduced to practice in his holy life, he taught also in word and by writing. He stands distinguished for exposing and destroying the lurking- places of unbelievers and Jansenists, so widely spread about. And, over and beyond this, he has cleared up questions that were clouded; he has solved what was doubtful, making a safe path, through which the directors of Christian souls may tread with foot unhurt, between the involved opinions of theologians, whether too loose or too rigorous.

Alphonsus Maria di Liguori may be adorned with the title and the honors of *Doctor of the Church."*

[6] The Saint who was declared a Doctor of the Church and who lived the closest in time to St. Alphonsus died in 1274, over five centuries earlier.

And besides this, he has signally cast light on the doctrines of the Immaculate Conception, and of the Infallibility of the Sovereign Pontiff teaching *ex cathedra*; and he strenuously taught these doctrines, which in our day have been defined as of faith.

He has, finally, made clear dark passages of the Holy Scriptures, both in his ascetic writings, which are freighted with a celestial odor, and in a most salutary commentary, in which, for the nourishment of piety and the instruction of the soul, he has given expositions of the Psalms, as well as of the hymns recited in the Divine Office, for the benefit especially of those obliged to its recitation.

Finally, from the original Preface to the Centenary Edition is included a letter from Pope Leo XIII to priests of the Congregation of the Most Holy Redeemer. In this, the Holy Father highlights how practical and approachable are the writings of St. Alphonsus. He said, "[St. Alphonsus] very well knew how to adapt Catholic truths to the comprehension of all, to provide for the moral direction of souls, to excite in a wonderful way true piety in the hearts of all … He has by means of numerous learned ascetical works enkindled, as it were, by burning coals, nourished and augmented languishing love principally toward our Lord Jesus Christ and His sweetest Mother, for whom, to the great advantage of the people, he knew how to inflame the coldest hearts." As a result, and, as he emphasized, "what is above all worthy of remark, though he wrote so many things, it must be acknowledged that, after an attentive examination, these writings may be read by the faithful without the least danger to their faith." Therefore, the Holy Father added, "Although the writings of the holy Doctor Alphonsus Maria de Liguori have already been spread throughout the world, not without very great profit to the Christian religion, yet it is desirable that they be propagated more and more, and be found in the hands of all."

~~~

It is for the latter reason, and for the reason of the manifold errors spread throughout the world today, as in the time of St. Alphonsus himself, that the works of St. Alphonsus must become known and read once again. Their orthodoxy, clarity, and accessibility, and their power to ignite within souls a great zeal for sanctity, make them invaluable gifts from Divine Providence. May this age of the world take them up and, by meditating on the eternal truths found in the school of this great Doctor, obtain their salvation and store up for themselves abundant treasures in Heaven.

The following presentations of *A Christian's Rule of Life* and *Darts of Fire* are entirely the original of St. Alphonsus Liguori. The only changes that have been made are to the layout and very occasional punctuations. Any further adjustments are noted in the footnotes. Footnotes that end with "- Ed" are original to the Centenary Edition. Footnotes with commentary from the publisher of this edition are marked as "- CDF".

After the presentation of *A Christian's Rule of Life*, I have compiled two *Summaries* of the wisdom and the counsel contained therein. Most of that presentation is my summary or paraphrasing of the words of the Saint, in which I made the attempt to capture the voice he uses in his writings. Anything presented in quotes is taken directly from *A Christian's Rule of Life*. The writings of St. Alphonsus contain, in the footnotes, the Latin text for all Scripture verses which he quotes. These are retained in this edition. The Latin text is from the Vulgate edition of the Bible, a greatly revered translation which the Church has relied upon since the time of St. Jerome.

<div style="text-align: right;">Charles D. Fraune</div>

A Christian's Rule of Life

This classic work of St. Alphonsus is from the Ascetical Works, Volume One:

*Preparation for Death
or, Considerations on the Eternal Truths.*

(Maxims of Eternity – Rule of Life.)

By
St. Alphonsus De Liguori
Doctor of the Church

Edited by
Rev. Eugene Grimm
Priest of the Congregation of the Most Holy Redeemer.

Nihil obstat: Arthur J. Scanlan, S.T.D., *Censor Librorum.*
Imprimatur: + Patritius Cardinalis Hayes, *Archiepiscopus Neo-Eboracensis*

Original Copyright 1926 by Very Rev. James Barron, C.SS.R.

INTRODUCTION

"A Christian's Rule of Life"

In 1816, just twenty-nine years after his death, Pope Pius VII said, "Alphonsus was in God's hands a sharp arrow, which, discharged against vice, strikes now in one place, now in another, in order to promote the honor of God and the salvation of souls. As a sharp arrow, heated by the fire of love, he has wounded the hearts of not a few priests ... One cannot wonder enough how many enmities he has removed, how many wandering sinners he has led back to the right road and to Christian perfection, by word and example, and by his numerous writings." Beginning within his own earthly life, his praise has been sung by the whole Church for centuries, meriting him the title "Doctor of the Church," and placing him among the greatest whom God has raised up in holiness for the salvation of souls and the glory of God.

In this present work, St. Alphonsus is at his finest, and to whom else should we turn than one such as him to understand more fully the necessary aspects of the life of a Christian. St. Alphonsus is so much more than a highly intelligent Catholic author; he was a faithful son of the Church from his youth, who learned early in his life that God must be the most loved in one's life; he was one of the greatest missionaries in the history of the Church, a zealous preacher and compassionate father and shepherd, who sought after the sheep that had long been neglected and were starving for Truth; he was a man of intense prayer and penance, most strict on himself but most compassionate to those who sought the Lord's mercy; he was a man gifted with countless miracles, signs proving his deep love and fidelity to our Blessed Lord.

The people of his time knew that he was singularly blessed with the graces needed for their age, in which the Church struggled against the rigorist and joyless Jansenist heresy. St. Alphonsus, in his tireless work for the glory of God and the salvation of souls, returned the Church to the joy of the Christian life which had been overshadowed by this deception of the enemy of souls. Our age is not unlike his. Today, Christians languish beneath a shroud of confusion, heresy, apostasy, materialism, and an infection of practical atheism among the leaders of the Church. It is in this age that we need a Saint such as Alphonsus, one who can both remind us of the essentials of the Faith, what must be believed and what must be done, but also stir our hearts, as only a Saint can do, to make the love of God our central desire and pursuit.

St. Alphonsus is at one and the same time severe and brimming over with joy at the nature and the promises of the Christian life. Salvation is ours to lay hold of, he would say, by embracing the love of God and loving Him in return. While there are serious obligations incumbent upon all men, the gifts and aids and assistance which Our Lord provides through His Holy Church are more than abundant. From the Sacraments to the Saints, with Our Lord and His Holy Mother ever at our side, the gates of Heaven are wide open and graces flow steadily upon all who turn to Jesus Christ to be saved.

In *A Christian's Rule of Life*, St. Alphonsus reminds us of the core practices, prayers, and perspectives that will propel us to Paradise. Those who follow the Christian rule of life have nothing to fear on that day when Our Lord calls them into eternal life. Let us heed the words of this great Saint and persevere in hope unto the end.

Charles D. Fraune

A CHRISTIAN'S RULE OF LIFE

By
St. Alphonsus Liguori

In this Rule the first chapter treats of the means we must make use of to keep ourselves in the grace of God. In the second, the acts of those devout exercises which should be practised are set forth at length. In the third is shown the exercise of the principal virtues which a Christian ought to practise.

"The Rule of Life" was published about the year 1767, in the volume entitled "The Way of Salvation," of which it formed the third part with the treatise called "Darts of Fire." In the general order of the works of Saint Alphonsus it naturally found its place under the title of the present volume (*Preparation for Death*) that contains the foundation of the spiritual life; it is the complement, the practical conclusion of the Considerations on the eternal truths, as the Author himself so very frequently intimates.[1]

---

[1] This paragraph was a footnote from the editor in the original work. - CDF

CHAPTER I

THE MEANS OF PRESERVING THE GRACE OF GOD

We must be fully persuaded that in order to obtain eternal salvation, it is not sufficient to wish to be saved; but we must further use the means which have been left us by Jesus Christ. Otherwise, if we commit sins, it will not avail us in the day of judgment to excuse ourselves by saying that the temptations were great, and we were weak; because God has given us the means, through his grace, to conquer all the assaults of our enemies: if, then, we do not take advantage of them, and are overcome, the fault will be our own. All men desire to be saved; but because they omit to employ the means of salvation, they sin and are lost.

§ 1. To Flee From the Occasions of Sin

The first means is to avoid all occasions of sin. It is impossible for any one who does not endeavor to flee from the occasions of sin, especially in the matter of sensual pleasures, to avoid falling into sin. St. Philip Neri said: "In the war of the senses, the conquerors are the *cowards* who fly." The occasion is like a veil put before our eyes, so that we can see nothing else – neither God, nor hell, nor the resolutions we had made. The Scripture says, it is impossible to walk on burning coals without being burnt: *Or can he walk upon hot coals, and his feet not be burnt?*[1] So it is morally impossible for any one to put himself voluntarily into the occasion of sin and not to fall, although he may have made a thousand resolutions and a thousand promises to God. This is clearly shown every day by the misery of so many poor souls who are plunged into vice for not avoiding the occasions. Any one who has had the evil habit of sins of impurity must know that, in order to restrain himself, it is not enough merely to avoid those occasions which are absolutely proximate; for if he does not also flee from those which are not altogether proximate,

---

[1] "Numquid potest homo . . . ambulare super prunas, ut non comburantur plant ejus?" – Prov. vi. 27.

he will easily fall again. Nor must we allow ourselves to be deceived by the devil into thinking that the person towards whom we are tempted is a saint; it often happens that the more devout a person is, the stronger is the temptation. St. Thomas Aquinas says, that the holiest persons attract the most. The temptation will begin in a spiritual way, and will terminate carnally. The great servant of God F. Sertorio Caputo, of the Society of Jesus, said that the devil first induces one to love a person's virtue, then the person, and then blinds one and brings one to ruin. We must also flee from evil companions: we are too weak; the devil is continually tempting us, and the senses are drawing us to evil; the slightest suggestion of a bad companion is only wanting to make us fall. Therefore the first thing that we have to do to save ourselves is to avoid evil occasions and bad companions. And we must in this matter do violence to ourselves, resolutely overcoming all human respect. Those who do not use violence to themselves will not be saved.[2] It is true, that we must not put confidence in our own strength, but only in the divine assistance; but God wills that we should do our part in doing violence to ourselves, when it is *necessary* to do so, in order to gain Paradise: *The violent bear it away.*[3]

---

[2] This is in reference to Matthew 11:12 which, the DR version, states: "And from the days of John the Baptist until now, the kingdom of heaven suffereth violence, and the violent bear it away." This means that only those who resist their fallen nature, do penance, embrace poverty, and are austere like St. John the Baptist, will be able to enter the Kingdom of Heaven and obtain their salvation. - CDF

[3] "Violenti rapiunt illud."—Matt. xi. 12.

§ 2. Mental Prayer

The second means is *mental prayer.* Without this, the soul will find it almost impossible to remain a long time in the grace of God. The Holy Spirit says: *In all thy works remember thy last end, and thou shalt never sin.*[1] He who often meditates on the Four Last Things, namely, death, judgment, and the eternity of hell and paradise, will not fall into sin. These truths are not to be seen with the [natural] eyes, but only with the eyes of the mind: if they are not meditated on, they vanish from the mind, and then the pleasures of the senses present themselves, and those who do not keep before themselves the eternal truths are easily taken up by them; and this is the reason why so many abandon themselves to vice, and are damned.

All Christians know and believe that all must die, and that we shall all be judged; but because they do not think about this, they live far from God. Without mental prayer there is no light; we walk in the dark; and walking in the dark, we do not see the danger which we are in, we do not make use of the means we ought, nor pray to God to help us, and so we are lost. Without prayer we have neither light nor

---

[1] "Memorare novissima tua, et in aeternum non peccabis." – Ecclus. vii. 40.

strength to advance in the ways of God; because without prayer we do not ask God to give us his grace, and without so praying we shall certainly fall. It was for this reason that Cardinal Bellarmine declared it to be morally impossible for a Christian who does not meditate to persevere in the grace of God. Whereas he who makes his meditation every day can scarcely fall into sin; and if unhappily he should fall on some occasion, by continuing his prayer he will return immediately to God.

It was said by a servant of God that "mental prayer and mortal sin cannot exist together." Resolve, then, to make every day, either in the morning or in the evening – but it is best in the morning – half an hour's meditation. In the following chapter you will see briefly explained an easy method for making this prayer.[2] For the rest, it is sufficient that during that time you should recollect yourself by reading some book of meditation – either this one or one of the many others; and from time to time excite some good affection or some aspiration, as you will find pointed out in the following chapter. Above all, I beg you never to leave off this prayer, which you should practise at least once a day, although you may be in great aridity, and should feel great weariness in performing it. If you do not discontinue it, you will certainly be saved.

Together with prayer, it is of great use to make a spiritual reading, in private, out of some book which treats of the life of a saint or of the Christian virtues, during half, or at least a quarter of an hour. How many by reading a pious book have changed their way of living and become saints! Like St. John Colombino, St. Ignatius Loyola, and so many others. It would also be a most useful thing if you were every year to make a retreat in some religious house. But at least do not omit your daily meditation.

---

[2] See page 24.

§ 3. The Frequentation of the Sacraments

The third means is *the frequenting of the sacraments of confession and of Communion*. By confession the soul keeps itself purified; and by it, it not only obtains remission of sins, but also greater strength to resist temptations. For this purpose you should choose a director, and always confess to the same, consulting him on all more important matters, even temporal ones; and obey him in everything, especially if you are distressed by scruples. He who obeys his confessor need not fear to go astray: *He that heareth you, heareth Me.*[1] The voice of the confessor is the voice of God.

Holy Communion is called heavenly bread, because as common bread preserves the life of the body, so Communion preserves the life of the soul: *Except you eat the flesh of the Son of Man ... you shall not have life in you.*[2] On the other hand, to those who often eat this bread eternal life is promised: *If any man eat of this bread, he shall live forever.*[3] Therefore the Council of Trent calls Holy Communion "the medicine which delivers us from venial sins and preserves us from mortal ones." You

---

[1] "Qui vos audit, me audit." – Luke, x. 16.
[2] "Nisi manducaveritis carnem Filii hominis, et biberitis ejus sanguinem, non habebitis vitam in vobis." – John, vi. 54.
[3] "Si quis manducaverit ex hoc pane, vivet in aeternum." – John, vi. 52.

should, then, resolve to go to Communion at least once a week, being determined not to give it up for anything in the world; as there is no affair of greater importance than that of your eternal salvation. Indeed, the longer you remain in the world, the greater need you have of assistance, because your temptations are greater.[4] To make a good confession, as also a good Communion, see the following chapter, where you will also find the acts which may be made before and after confession and Communion by way of preparation and thanksgiving.[5]

---

[4] A certain learned priest wrote three books against the opinion which I had maintained, namely, that a person who desires to keep himself in the grace of God may be allowed to communicate every week, although he may not be purified from the affection to venial sins. On this matter, I beg the reader to read the last answer in my "Moral Instruction," lately printed. (See opuscule entitled "Frequent Communion."). CDF note: the work referenced here is not contained in this present book.

[5] Page 28.

§ 4. To Hear Mass

The fourth means is to *hear Mass* every day.[1] When we attend Mass we give more honor to God than all the angels and saints in heaven can give him, because theirs is the honor of creatures; but in the Mass we offer to God Jesus Christ, who gives him an infinite honor. Read the following chapter, where you will also find a way of hearing Mass with much profit.[2]

---

[1] "Hearing Mass" means attending Mass, with a devout focus being implied. - CDF
[2] Page 35.

§ 5. The Visit to the Most Holy Sacrament & to the Blessed Virgin

The fifth means is to *make a visit every day to the Most Holy Sacrament in some church, and to the Divine Mother*[1] before some devout image. Jesus Christ dwells on the altars of so many churches in order to dispense graces to all who come to visit him; and thus the souls of those who practise this beautiful devotion receive innumerable benefits from it. At the end of the next chapter you will find the prayer which may be said when visiting the Most Holy Sacrament and the Divine Mother.[2] The graces you ought especially to ask for, both from Jesus and Mary, are the love of God and holy perseverance till death.

---

[1] "Divine Mother" is a pious Catholic expression that simply means "Mother of God." The Blessed Virgin Mary is the mother of a Divine Person.- CDF

[2] Beginning on page 37.

§ 6. Prayer

The sixth means which I recommend you above all to put in practice is *holy prayer*. It is certain that without the divine assistance we can do nothing good for our souls. God also has declared that graces are granted to those only who ask for them: *Ask, and it shall be given you.*[1] Seek, and it shall be given you; therefore, as says St. Teresa, he who seeks not does not receive. Hence it is a common opinion of the holy Fathers, with St. Thomas, that without prayer it is impossible to persevere in the grace of God, and to save one's self. But he who prays is sure of the help of God; we have his word for it, which cannot fail, repeated so often in the sacred Gospels: *All things whatsoever you ask when ye pray, believe that you shall receive, and they shall come to you.*[2] *Every one that asketh receiveth.*[3] *Amen, amen, I say unto you, if you ask the Father anything in My name, He will give it you.*[4] God grants everything that we ask him for in the name of Jesus Christ. If, then, we wish to be

---

[1] "Petite, et dabitur vobis." – Matt. vii. 7.
[2] "Omnia quaecumque orantes petitis, credite quia accipietis, et evenient vobis." – Mark xi. 24.
[3] "Omnis enim qui petit, accipit." – Luke xi. 10.
[4] "Amen, amen, dico vobis: si quid petieritis Patrem in nomine meo, dabit vobis." – John xvi. 23.

saved, we must pray, and pray with humility and confidence, and above all with perseverance. And this is the reason why mental prayer is so useful, because then we are reminded to pray; otherwise we forget to do so, and so are lost. St. Teresa says, that out of her desire of seeing every one saved, she would have wished to go to the top of a mountain and then to cry out, so as to be heard by all men, nothing but these words, "Pray! pray!" The ancient Fathers of the desert in their conferences decided that there was no better means of saving ourselves than by continually repeating the prayer of David: *Incline unto my aid, O God! O Lord, make haste to help me!*[5] So let us also try to say. Or else let us make use of the beautiful ejaculation of the Blessed F. Leonard of Porto-Maurice: "'My Jesus, mercy!" And the two principal graces which we must always ask for (as I have said before), are the love of God and holy perseverance. We must always ask the same graces from the Most Holy Mary, who is called the dispenser of all the divine graces; and when we pray to her, she will certainly obtain them for us from God. Therefore St. Bernard thus exhorts us: "Let us seek grace, and let us seek it through Mary; for what she seeks she finds, and she cannot be disappointed."[6]

---

[5] "Deus, in adjutorium meum intende; Domine, ad adjuvandum me festina." – Ps. lxix. 2.
[6] Queramus gratiam, et per Mariam queramus; quia, quod querit, invenit, et frustrari non potest.

CHAPTER II

ACTS & PRACTICES OF PIETY

§ 1. Acts & Different Prayers on Rising in the Morning, & During the Day

On rising make the sign of the cross, and then say:

My God, I adore Thee and love Thee with all my heart.

I thank Thee for all Thy benefits, and especially for having preserved me this night.

I offer Thee whatever I may do or suffer this day, in union with the actions and sufferings of Jesus and of Mary, with the intention of gaining all the indulgences I can gain.

I resolve to avoid all sin this day, and especially such a one (*it is good to make a resolution, particularly about the fault into which we fall the oftenest*); and I beg of Thee to give me perseverance for the love of Jesus Christ.

I resolve to conform myself to Thy holy will, and particularly in those things that are contrary to my inclination, saying always: Lord, Thy will be done.

My Jesus! keep Thy hand over me this day. Most Holy Mary! take me beneath thy mantle. And do Thou, Eternal Father, help me, for the love of Jesus and Mary! O my angel guardian and my patron saints, assist me.

[Say] an *Our Father* and a *Hail Mary* and the *Creed*, with three *Hail Marys* in honor of the purity of Mary.

~~~~~

When you begin any work or study, say:
Lord! I offer Thee this work.

When you eat:
My God, bless this food and me, that I may commit no fault about it;[1] and may all be for Thy glory.

After having eaten:
I thank Thee, Lord! for having done good to one who was Thy enemy.

When the clock strikes:
My Jesus! I love Thee: never permit me to offend Thee again, and let me never be separated from Thee.

In adverse circumstances:
Lord, since Thou hast so willed it, I will it also.

In time of temptation often repeat:
Jesus and Mary!

When you know or doubt of some fault or sin you have committed, say immediately:
My God! I repent of having offended Thee, O Infinite Goodness! I will do so no more.

And if it was a grievous sin, confess it at once.

~~~~~

---

[1] In the Church's tradition of the use of Sacramentals, the blessing at meals, and the blessing of various foods, is, in part, a request that God moderate our appetite and our use of the food, that we may not sin while eating.- CDF

It would be a good thing for parents and masters and mistresses to make the children and those under them learn these acts by heart, that they may use them afterwards throughout life.

§ 2. Method of Making Mental Prayer

Mental prayer consists of three parts; the *preparation*, the *meditation*, and the *conclusion*.

The preparation consists of three acts: one of *faith* in the presence of God; of *humility*, with a short act of contrition; and of *prayer to be enlightened*: saying as follows:

For the first (faith):

My God, I believe that Thou art present with me, and I adore Thee with all the affection of my soul.

For the second (humility):

O Lord, by my sins I deserve to be now in hell; I repent, O Infinite Goodness! with my whole heart, of having offended Thee.

For the third (prayer):

My God, for the love of Jesus and Mary, give me light in this prayer, that I may profit by it.

Then say a *Hail Mary* to the Most Blessed Virgin, that she may obtain light for us; and a *Glory be to the Father*, to St. Joseph, to your guardian angel, and to your patron saint, for the same end. These acts should be made with attention, but briefly; and then you go on directly to the meditation.

In the *meditation* you can always make use of some book,[1] at least at the beginning, and stop where you find yourself mostly touched. St. Francis de Sales says that in this we should do as the bees, which settle on a flower as long they find any honey in it, and then pass on to another. It should also be observed, that the fruits to be gained by meditation are three in number: *to make affections, to pray, and to make resolutions*; and in these consists the profit to be derived from mental prayer.

After you have meditated on some eternal truth, and God has spoken to your heart, you must also speak to God; and first, by forming *affections*, be they acts of faith, of thanksgiving, of humility, or of hope; but above all, repeat the

---

[1] Here it may be well to mention what the Author himself wrote to his religious, in a circular dated February 26, 1771: "I recommend that for the most part the meditation should be made from my books: *The Preparation for Death, Meditation on the Passion, Darts of Fire,* which are in the WAY OF SALVATION; and *Meditations for Advent,* up to the *Octave of Epiphany.* I say this, not in order to put forward my own poor books, but because these meditations are made up of devout affections, and what is of more importance, are full of holy prayer, of which I do not find many in other books. And hence I beg that the second part of the Meditation, consisting of affections and prayers, be always read."

We must observe that Saint Alphonsus makes the practice of mental prayer simple, clear, easy, and not less fruitful. Owing to the method which he teaches, this exercise, indispensable to him who wishes to sanctify himself, is really put within the reach of all. He wishes that every one should learn how to meditate. He earnestly recommends that for this purpose special instructions should be given to the people.

Pope Benedict XIV grants to those who in a church or elsewhere, either in public or private, shall teach the manner of making mental prayer, as well as to those who attend such instruction, a plenary indulgence once a month, on the day on which they confess and communicate and pray to the intention of the Church; likewise an indulgence of seven years and seven times forty days, each time when, having been truly contrite, and having communicated, they teach mental prayer or attend an explanation that is given to learn how to make it. These indulgences are applicable to the souls in purgatory. – Ed.

acts of love and contrition. St. Thomas says that every act of love merits for us the grace of God and paradise: "Every act of love merits eternal life."[2] Each act of contrition obtains the same thing. Acts of love are such as these: *My God, I love Thee above all things! I love Thee with all my heart! I desire to do Thy will in all things. I rejoice that Thou art infinitely happy!* and the like. For an act of contrition it is enough to say: *O Infinite Goodness, I repent of having offended Thee!*

In the second place, you must *pray*; ask God to enlighten you, to give you humility or other virtues, to grant you a good death and eternal salvation; but above all, his love and holy perseverance. And when the soul is in great aridity, it is sufficient to repeat: *My God, help me! Lord, have mercy on me! My Jesus, have mercy!* and if you do nothing but this, your prayer will succeed exceedingly well.

In the third place, before finishing your prayer, you must form a particular *resolution*; as, for instance, to avoid some occasion of sin, to bear with an annoyance from some person, to correct some fault, and the like.

Finally, in the *conclusion*, three acts are to be made: in the 1st, we must thank God for the inspirations we have received; in the 2nd, we must make a determination to observe the resolutions we have made; in the 3rd, we must ask God, for the love of Jesus and Mary, to help us to keep our resolution. The prayer concludes by the recommendation of the souls in purgatory, the prelates of the Church, sinners, and all our relatives and friends, for which we may say an *Our Father* and a *Hail Mary*. St. Francis de Sales exhorts us to choose some thought which may have struck us more especially in our prayer, that we may remember it during the rest of the day.

Benedict XIV granted seven years' indulgence to those who make half or at least a quarter of an hour's mental prayer during the day,

---

[2] "Quilibet actus charitatis meretur vitam eternam." – I, 2, q. 114, a. 7, ad 3.

and a plenary indulgence if it is made every day for a month, on the condition of confession and Communion.[3]

---

[3] In the modern *Manual of Indulgences*, this is stated as simply as "one may gain a partial indulgence by engaging in mental prayer." - CDF

§ 3. Acts to be Made by Way of Preparation & Thanksgiving Both for Confession & Communion

Before confessing, the penitent should beg for light from God to enable him to know what sins he has committed, and to obtain the grace of a true sorrow and purpose of amendment. He should also particularly recommend himself to Our Lady of Sorrows, that she may obtain contrition for him. Then he may make the following acts:

Act before Confession

O God of infinite majesty, behold at Thy feet a traitor, who has offended Thee over and over again, but who now humbly seeks forgiveness. O Lord, reject me not; Thou dost not despise a heart that humbles itself: *A contrite and humbled heart, O God, Thou wilt not despise.*[1] I thank Thee that Thou hast waited for me till now, and hast not let me die in sin, casting me into hell, as I deserved. Since Thou hast waited

---

[1] "Cor contritum et humiliatum, Deus, non despicies." – Ps. 1. 19.

for me, my God, I hope that, by the merits of Jesus Christ, Thou wilt pardon me in this confession for all the offences I have committed against Thee; I repent, and am sorry for them, because by them I have merited hell and lost paradise. But above all, it is not so much on account of hell which I have merited, but because I have offended Thee, O Infinite Goodness! that I am sorry from the bottom of my heart. I love Thee, O Sovereign Good! and because I love Thee, I repent of all the insults I have offered Thee. I have turned my back upon Thee; I have not respected Thee; I have despised Thy grace and Thy friendship. O Lord! I have lost Thee by my own free-will; forgive me all my sins for the love of Jesus Christ, now that I repent with all my heart; I hate, detest, and abominate them above every evil. And I repent not only of mortal sins, but also of venial sins, because these are also displeasing to Thee. I resolve for the future, by Thy grace, never more wilfully to offend Thee. Yes, my God, I will rather die than ever sin again.

And if a person confesses a sin into which he has often relapsed, it is a good thing to resolve particularly not to fall into it again, by promising to avoid the occasion of it, and to take the means pointed out by the confessor, or such as he may himself judge to be most efficacious for correcting himself of it.

Act after Confession

My dear Jesus! how much do I not owe Thee. By the merits of Thy blood I hope that I have this day been pardoned. I thank Thee above all things. I hope to reach heaven, where I shall praise Thy mercies forever. My God, if I have hitherto lost Thee so often, I now desire to lose Thee no more. From this day forward I will change my life in earnest. Thou dost merit all my love; I will love Thee truly; I will no longer see myself separated from Thee, I have promised Thee this already; now I repeat my promise of being ready to die rather than offend Thee again. I promise also to avoid all occasions of sin, and to use such means as will prevent me from falling again. My Jesus, Thou knowest my weakness: give me grace to be faithful to Thee till death, and to have recourse to Thee when I am tempted. Most holy Mary, help me! Thou art the mother of perseverance; I place my hope in thee.

Preparation for Communion

There is no means more efficacious in freeing us from our sins, and in enabling us to advance in the love of God, than Holy Communion. Why is it, then, that some souls find themselves always in the same tepidity, and committing the same faults, notwithstanding the many Communions they make? This happens through the want of a proper disposition and preparation. Two things are requisite for this preparation. The first is to disengage our heart from all affections which are an impediment to the divine love. The second is to have a great desire to love God. And this, says St. Francis de Sales, should be our chief intention when we communicate, namely, to increase in divine love. Out of love alone, says the saint, ought our God to be received, who out of love alone gives himself to us. For this end let us make the following acts.

Acts before Communion

My beloved Jesus, true Son of God, who didst die for me on the cross in a sea of sorrow and ignominy, I firmly believe that Thou art present in the Most Holy Sacrament; and for this faith I am ready to give my life.

My dear Redeemer, I hope by Thy goodness, and through the merits of Thy blood, that when Thou dost come to me this morning, Thou wilt inflame me with Thy holy love, and wilt give me all those graces which I need to keep me obedient and faithful to Thee till death.

Ah, my God! true and only lover of my soul, what couldst Thou do more to oblige me to love Thee? Thou wert not satisfied, my love, with dying for me, but Thou wouldst also institute the Most Holy Sacrament, making Thyself my food, and giving Thyself all to me; thus uniting Thyself most closely to such a miserable and ungrateful creature. Thou dost Thyself invite me to receive Thee, and dost greatly desire that I should receive Thee. O infinite Love! A God gives himself all to me! O my God, O infinite love, worthy of infinite love, I love Thee above all things; I love Thee with all my heart; I love Thee more than myself, more than my life; I love Thee because Thou art worthy of being loved; and I love Thee also to please Thee, since Thou dost desire my love! Depart from my soul, all ye earthly affections; to Thee alone, my Jesus, my treasure, my all, will I give all my love. This morning Thou dost give Thyself all to me, and I give myself all to Thee. Permit me to love Thee; for I desire none but Thee, and nothing but what is pleasing to Thee. I love Thee, O my Saviour, and I unite my poor love to the love of all the angels and saints, and of Thy Mother Mary, and the love of Thy Eternal Father! Oh, that I could see Thee loved by all! Oh, that I could make Thee loved by all men, and loved as much as Thou dost deserve!

Behold, O my Jesus, I am now about to draw near to feed on Thy most sacred Flesh! Ah, my God, who am I? and who art Thou? Thou art a Lord of infinite goodness, and I am a loathsome worm, defiled by so many sins, and who have driven Thee out of my soul so often.

Domine, non sum dignus. Lord, I am not worthy to remain in Thy presence; I ought to be in hell forever, far away, and abandoned by Thee. But out of Thy goodness Thou callest me to receive Thee: behold, I come, I come humbled and in confusion for the great displeasure I have given Thee, but trusting entirely to Thy mercy and to the love Thou hast for me. I am exceedingly sorry, O my loving Redeemer, for having so often offended Thee in time past! Thou didst even give Thy life for me; and I have so often despised Thy grace and Thy love, and have exchanged Thee for nothing. I repent, and am sorry with all my heart for every offence which I have offered Thee, whether grievous or light, because it was an offence against Thee, who art infinite goodness, I hope Thou hast already pardoned me; but if Thou hast not yet forgiven me, pardon me, my Jesus, before I receive Thee. Ah, receive me quickly into Thy grace, since it is Thy will soon to come and dwell within me.

Come, then, my Jesus, come into my soul, that sighs after Thee. My only and infinite good, my life, my love, my all, I would desire to receive Thee this morning with the same love with which those souls who love Thee most have received Thee, and with the same fervor with which Thy Most Holy Mother received Thee; to her Communions I wish to unite this one of mine. O Blessed Virgin, and my Mother Mary, give me Thy Son; I intend to receive him from thy hands! Tell him that I am thy servant, and thus will he press me more lovingly to his heart now that he is coming to me.

Acts after Communion

The time after Communion is a precious time for gaining treasures of grace, because the acts and prayers made whilst the soul is thus united with Jesus Christ have more merit, and are of more value, than when they are made at any other time. St. Teresa says that our Lord then dwells in the soul enthroned as on a mercy-seat, and speaks to it in these words: *My child, ask of me what you will; for this end am I come to you, to do you good.* Oh, what great favors do those receive who converse with Jesus Christ after Communion! The Ven. F. Avila never omitted to remain two hours in prayer after Communion; and St. Aloysius Gonzaga continued his thanksgiving for three days. Let the communicant, then, make the following acts, and try during the rest of the day to go on making acts of love and prayer, in order to keep himself united with Jesus Christ, whom he has received in the morning.

~~~~~

Behold, my Jesus, Thou art come, Thou art now within me, and hast made Thyself all mine. Be Thou welcome, my Beloved Redeemer. I adore Thee, and cast myself at Thy feet; I embrace Thee, I press Thee to my heart, and thank Thee for that Thou hast deigned to enter into my breast. O Mary, O my patron saints, O my guardian angel, do you all thank him for me! Since then, O my Divine King! Thou art come to visit me with so much love, I give Thee my will, my liberty, and my whole self. Thou hast given Thyself all to me, I will give myself all to Thee; I will no longer belong to myself; from this day forward I will be Thine, and altogether Thine. I desire that my soul, my body, my faculties, my senses, should be all Thine, that they may be employed in serving and pleasing Thee. To Thee I consecrate all my thoughts, my desires, my affections, and all my life. I have offended Thee enough, my Jesus; I desire to spend the remainder of my life in loving Thee, who hast loved me so much.

Accept, O God of my soul, the sacrifice which I, a miserable sinner, make to Thee, and who desires only to love and please Thee. Work Thou in me, and dispose of me, and of all things belonging to me, as Thou pleasest. May Thy love destroy in me all those affections which are displeasing to Thee, that I may be all Thine, and may live only to please Thee!

I ask Thee not for goods of this world, for pleasures, for honors; give me, I pray Thee, by the merits of Thy Passion, O my Jesus, a constant sorrow for my sins! Enlighten me, and make me know the vanity of worldly goods, and how much Thou dost deserve to be loved. Separate me from all attachment to the world, and bind me entirely to Thy love, that from henceforth my will may neither seek nor desire anything but what Thou willest. Give me patience and resignation in infirmities, in poverty, and in all those things which are contrary to my self-love. Make me gentle towards those who despise me. Give me a holy death. Give me Thy holy love. And, above all, I pray Thee to give me perseverance in Thy grace till death; never permit me to separate myself from Thee again: *Jesu dulcissime, ne permittas me separari a Te.* And I also ask of Thee the grace always to have recourse to Thee, and to invoke Thy aid, O my Jesus, in all my temptations; and the grace to ask Thee always for holy perseverance.

O Eternal Father, Thy Son Jesus Christ has promised me that Thou wilt grant me everything that I shall ask Thee in his name: *If you ask the Father anything in My name, He will give it you.*[2] In the name, therefore, and by the merits of this Son, I ask for Thy love and holy perseverance, that I may one day love Thee in heaven with all my strength, and sing Thy mercies forever, secure of never more being separated from Thee.

O most holy Mary, my mother and my hope, obtain for me these graces which I so desire; as also a great love for thee, my Queen: may I always recommend myself to thee in all my necessities!

---

[2] "Si quid petieritis Patrem in nomine meo, dabit vobis." – John xvi. 23.

§ 4. Method of Hearing Mass

The same action is performed in the Mass as was accomplished on Calvary, except that there the blood of Jesus Christ was really shed, while on the altar it is shed mystically; but in the Mass the merits of the Passion of Jesus are applied to each one in particular. To hear Mass, therefore, with great fruit, we must pay attention to the ends for which it was instituted, namely: 1. To honor God. 2. To thank him for his benefits. 3. To satisfy for our sins. 4. To obtain graces. For this reason you may use the following prayer during Mass.[1]

~~~~~

---

[1] Saint Alphonsus speaks here only of the two essential or principal points. "To satisfy the obligation of hearing Mass," he elsewhere says, "two things are necessary – an intention and attention. It is certain that those attending Mass offer the Holy Sacrifice with the priest. Think, therefore, of the great action which you perform. Meditate on the Passion of Jesus Christ, the Last Things, etc. If you prefer, read some spiritual book, or recite either the Office of the Blessed Virgin, or the Rosary, or other prayers. But at least pay attention to what the priest does." (Instr. on the Commandments, chap. 3.) – ED.

Eternal Father, in this Sacrifice I offer to Thee Thy Son Jesus, with all the merits of his Passion: 1. In honor of Thy majesty. 2. In thanksgiving for all the favors Thou hast hitherto shown me, and for all those which I hope to receive for all eternity. 3. In satisfaction for my sins, and for those of all the living and dead. 4. To obtain eternal salvation, and all the graces that are necessary for me to gain it.

At the elevation of the Host:
My God, for the love of this Thy Son, pardon me and give me holy perseverance.

At the elevation of the Chalice:
By the Blood of Jesus, give me Thy love and a holy death.

At the Communion of the priest, make a spiritual Communion saying:
My Jesus, I love Thee, and desire to possess Thee. I embrace Thee, and I will never more separate myself from Thee.

§ 5. Acts to be Made in Visiting the Most Holy Sacrament & the Divine Mother

My Lord Jesus Christ, who, for the love Thou bearest to mankind, dost remain night and day in this Sacrament, full of pity and love, awaiting, calling, and receiving all who come to visit Thee; I believe that Thou art present in the Sacrament of the Altar; I adore Thee from the depths of my own nothingness; I thank Thee for the many graces Thou hast given me, and especially for having given me Thyself in this Sacrament; for having given me Mary Thy Mother as my advocate, and for having called me to visit Thee in this church. I salute Thy most amiable and most loving heart; and I do so, first, in thanksgiving for this great gift; secondly, to atone for all the insults Thou hast received in this Sacrament from all infidels, heretics, and bad Catholics; thirdly, I intend in this visit to adore Thee in all those places where Thou, thus veiled in the Most Holy Sacrament, art least reverenced and most abandoned.

My Jesus, I love Thee with my whole heart. I am sorry that I have hitherto so often offended Thy infinite goodness. With the help of Thy grace, I resolve to displease Thee no more; and, unworthy as I am, I now consecrate myself wholly to Thee; I renounce and give to Thee my will, my affections, my desires, and all that is mine. Henceforward do with me, and all that belongs to me, whatsoever Thou pleasest. I ask for nothing but Thee and Thy holy love, final perseverance, and a perfect fulfilment of Thy will. I recommend to Thee the souls in purgatory, especially those who were most devout to this Most Holy Sacrament, and to Most Holy Mary. I also recommend to Thee all poor sinners. And lastly, my beloved Saviour, I unite all my affections to those of Thy most loving heart; and thus united, I offer them to Thy Eternal Father; and in Thy name I beseech him to accept and grant them.

While Visiting any Image of the Ever-Blessed Virgin

Most holy immaculate Virgin Mary, my Mother, I, the most miserable of sinners, have this day recourse to thee, the Mother of my Lord, the Queen of the universe, the advocate, the hope, the refuge of sinners! I worship[1] thee, O great Queen, and I thank thee for the many favors thou hast hitherto obtained for me; especially for having delivered me from Hell, which I have so often deserved. I love thee, O most amiable Lady, worthy of all love! and for the love I bear thee, I promise to serve thee always, and to do everything in my power to make others serve thee also. In thee do I hope; I place my salvation in thy hands. Accept me for thy servant, receive me under thy mantle, O Mother of Mercy! Thou art all-powerful with God; free me, then, from all temptations, or at least obtain for me strength to conquer them as long as I live. From thee I beg a true love of Jesus Christ; and by thy help I hope for a good death. I beseech thee, Mother, by the love thou bearest to God, that thou wilt always help me, but especially at the last moment of my life. Leave me not till thou shalt see me safe in heaven, blessing thee, and singing thy mercies for all eternity. Amen. This is my hope. So may it be!

---

[1] "Worship" here is an archaic English term which means "to honor." It is not intended to ascribe divinity to the one to whom it is used. – CDF

§ 6. Christian Acts, to be Made in the Evening Before Going to Bed

Before going to rest, make your examination of conscience in the following manner: First, thank God for all the favors you have received; then cast a glance over all the actions you have done and the words you have spoken during the day, repenting of all the faults you have committed. Afterwards make the Christian acts in the following manner:

~~~~~

Act of Faith

O my God, who art infallible truth, because Thou hast revealed it to Thy Church, I believe all that she proposes to my belief! I believe that Thou art my God, the Creator of all things; that Thou dost reward the just with an eternal paradise, and dost punish the wicked in hell for all eternity. I believe that Thou art one in essence, and three in persons, namely, Father, Son, and Holy Ghost. I believe in the Incarnation and death of Jesus Christ. I believe, in fine, all that the Holy Church believes. I thank Thee for having made me a Christian; and I protest that I will live and die in this holy faith.

Act of Hope

O my God, confiding in Thy promises, because Thou art powerful, faithful, and merciful, I hope through the merits of Jesus Christ to obtain pardon of my sins, final perseverance, and the glory of paradise.

Act of Love and Contrition

O my God, because Thou art infinite goodness, worthy of infinite love, I love Thee with all my heart above all things; and for the love of Thee I love my neighbor also. I repent with all my heart, and am sorry above all things for all my sins, because by them I have offended Thy infinite goodness. I resolve, by the help of Thy grace, which I beseech Thee to grant me now and always, rather to die than ever to offend Thee again. I purpose, also, to receive the holy Sacraments during my life, and at the hour of my death.

~~~~~

It is well to know, that to those who make these Christian acts with the desire of receiving the holy Sacraments during their life and at their death, Benedict XIII granted seven years' indulgence; and a plenary indulgence, applicable to the souls in purgatory, when they are said regularly for a month; as also a plenary indulgence in *articulo mortis* – at the hour of death. Besides, by a concession of Benedict XIV, the indulgence may be gained several times a day by any one who recites the above acts, provided he does so with the intention of gaining the indulgence.

Conclude the whole by saying the Rosary and the litany of the Blessed Virgin.

§ 7. Devout Prayers to Jesus & Mary to Obtain the Graces Necessary for Salvation

Prayer to Jesus Christ, to obtain His Holy Love

My crucified Jesus, I confess Thee to be the true Son of God and my Saviour. I adore and thank Thee for the death Thou didst suffer for me. My dear Redeemer, if I have hitherto done nothing but offend Thee, I am now sorry for it above all things, and I desire nothing but to love Thee. Thou hast promised to hear those who pray to Thee; by the merits of Thy Passion, I ask Thee to give me Thy holy love. Ah, draw my heart entirely to Thyself, that from this day forward I may love Thee with all my strength, and may love none other but Thee; and so may I one day come to love Thee for all eternity in paradise.

Prayer to obtain Final Perseverance

O sovereign and eternal God, I thank Thee for having created me; for having redeemed me by means of Jesus Christ; for having made me a Christian by calling me to the true faith, and giving me time to repent after the many sins I have committed. O Infinite Goodness, I love Thee above all things; and I repent with all my heart of all my offences against Thee. I hope Thou hast already pardoned me; but I am continually in danger of again offending Thee. For the love of Jesus Christ, I beg of Thee holy perseverance till death. Thou knowest my weakness; help me, then, and permit me never again to separate myself from Thee. Rather let me die a thousand times, than ever again to lose Thy grace. O Mary, my Mother, obtain for me holy perseverance!

Prayers to the Blessed Virgin Mary for Every Day in the Week

SUNDAY

To Obtain the Pardon of Sins

Behold at thy feet, O mother of God! a miserable sinner, who has recourse to thee, and places his confidence in thee. O Mother of mercy, have pity on me. Thou art the refuge, the hope of sinners; thou art, therefore, my refuge and my hope. Thou hast it in thy power to save me by thy holy intercession; succor me for the love of Jesus Christ, stretch forth thy hand to a fallen sinner who commends himself to thee. I know that thou delightest to assist a poor sinner; assist me therefore now that thou hast it in thy power to assist me. I have forfeited divine grace and lost my soul by my sins; I now put myself into thy hands; tell me what I must do to regain the grace of my Lord, for I am willing to do all that thou shalt direct me. To thee then do I have recourse. Thou prayest for many others, pray also to Jesus for me; ask him to pardon me, and he will pardon me; tell him that thou desirest my salvation and he will save me. Manifest the good which thou art able to accomplish in behalf of those who confide in thee. This is my hope. Amen.

MONDAY

To Obtain Holy Perseverance

O Queen of heaven, I dedicate myself to thee to be thy perpetual servant, and I offer myself to serve thee during my whole life; accept of me, and do not reject me as I have deserved. O mother, in thee do I place all my hopes. I bless and thank God, that, in his mercy, he has given me this confidence in thee, which I hold as a great earnest of my salvation. Ah, how have I hitherto miserably fallen, because I have not had recourse to thee! I now hope, through the merits of Jesus and thy prayers, that I have been pardoned; but I may again fall and forfeit divine grace. Most blessed Lady, protect me, and suffer me not to become any more the slave of the devil; always assist me; I know that thou wilt assist me, and I shall conquer with thy assistance, if I recommend myself to thee; but of this I am not afraid: I am afraid that when in danger of falling I may not call upon thee, and may perish. This favor I ask of thee, that in all the assaults of the devil I may always have recourse to thee, saying, Mary, help me; help me, Mary, most holy mother; do not suffer me to lose God.

TUESDAY

To Obtain a Happy Death

O Mary! what will my death be? Considering my sins, and reflecting on that awful moment, when I must breathe my last and be judged, I tremble and am confounded. Most holy Mother, in the blood of Jesus and in thy prayers are placed my hopes. O consolation of the afflicted, do not abandon me then; fail not to console me in that great affliction. If thou assist me not I shall be lost. Ah, blessed Lady! before my death be at hand, obtain for me a great sorrow for my sins, a real amendment of life and fidelity to God, during the remainder of my days. And when I shall arrive at the end of my life, O Mary, my hope, assist me in that distressing moment, and so comfort me that I may not fall into despair at the sight of my sins, which the devil will place before me. Grant that I may invoke thee then more frequently, and that I may expire with thy name on my tongue and the name of thy most holy and divine Son. O blessed Lady, pardon my assurance; but before I die, do thou in person come to console me with thy presence. I am a sinner, it is true, and do not deserve such a favor; but I am devoted to thee, I love thee, and have great confidence in thee. O Mary, I look for thee; let me not remain disconsolate. At least, if I be not then worthy of so great a favor, assist me from heaven, that I may depart from this life loving God and thee, to come to love thee eternally in heaven.

WEDNESDAY

To Escape Hell

Most dear and blessed Lady, I thank thee for having so often preserved me from falling into hell, which I have deserved by my repeated sins. Alas! there was a time when I must have stood condemned to that dreadful prison; and it may be that on my first committing sin the sentence would have been executed upon me had not thou in thy pity assisted me. Although I did not pray to thee, yet, through thy goodness alone, thou didst restrain divine justice; and conquering the hardness of my heart, induce me to place my confidence in thee. And oh! into how many more sins should I have fallen, to the dangers of which I was exposed, hadst not thou, my most affectionate Mother, preserved me from them by the graces which thou didst obtain for me! O holy Queen, continue, I beseech Thee, to preserve me from hell. If at one time I did not love thee, now, next to God, I love thee above all things. Never suffer me to turn my back upon thee, and upon God, who through thy means hast bestowed so many mercies upon me. Most amiable Lady, suffer me not to have to curse thee for all eternity in hell. Couldst thou endure to see one lost who is thy servant and loves thee? Most Blessed Virgin, since thou hast done so much to save me, accomplish thy work, and continue to assist me. But if thou, when I lived forgetful of thee, didst so favor me, what may I not expect from thee now that I love thee and recommend myself to thee! No, no one can be lost who recommends himself to thee. O my Mother, leave me not to myself, that I may be lost; grant that I may always have recourse to thee. Save me, my hope, by thy powerful intercession; save me from hell; and first save me from sin, which alone can condemn me to hell.

THURSDAY

To Obtain Heaven

O Queen of heaven, who sittest above all the choirs of angelic spirits nearest to the throne of God, from this valley of tears I salute thee, miserable sinner as I am, and beseech thee to turn towards me those eyes of mercy which distribute favors whithersoever thou directest them. Behold, O Mary! to how many dangers I am now exposed, and must remain exposed so long as I continue in this world, of losing my soul, heaven, and God. In thee, O blessed Lady! next to God, are placed all my hopes. I love thee, and long to approach and behold and praise thee in heaven. O Mary! when will the day come when I shall see myself saved at thy feet, and shall behold thee the mother of my Lord, and my mother also, who hast taken such pains to save me! O blessed Lady! I have been very ungrateful to thee during my life; but if I gain heaven, I shall not be any more ungrateful to thee: then shall I love thee as much as I am able for all eternity, and shall make amends for my past neglect by blessing thee, and thanking thee forever. I give sovereign thanks to God for having given me so great confidence in the blood of Jesus, and in thee, as to hope that thou wilt deliver me from my sins, and obtain for me light and strength to accomplish the divine will, and finally conduct me to the gates of paradise. Thy servants have very much hoped in thee, and none have been deceived; nor shall I be deceived. O Mary! thou desirest nothing else in my regard; thou wilt save me. Pray to thy Son Jesus (as I now beseech him through the merits of his bitter Passion) to preserve and to increase in me more and more this my confidence in thee, and I shall be saved.

FRIDAY

To Obtain Love for Jesus Christ and for Mary

O Mary! I know that thou art the most noble, the most holy, and the most amiable of all creatures. O blessed Lady! would that all knew thee and loved thee as thou deservest! I am consoled that so many holy souls both in heaven and on earth love thy goodness and beauty. Above all, I rejoice that God himself loves thee more than all men and angels. Most amiable Queen, I, a miserable sinner, also love thee, but I love thee too little; I desire to obtain a greater and more tender love for thee; obtain this for me: for to love thee is a great sign of predestination, and a grace which God does not grant but to those whom he especially wills to be saved. I am sensible, O holy Mother! that I am under immense obligations to thy Son, and he is deserving of infinite love. Thou desirest nothing else but to see him loved: to do this is the grace which above all others I beseech thee to obtain for me: obtain for me a great love for Jesus Christ. Thou obtainest from God whatever thou pleasest; oh, then, obtain for me the grace of being so united with the divine will that I may never be separated from it. I ask thee not for the goods of this world, nor for honors, nor riches; I ask thee for what thy heart most desires, that I may love my God. Is it possible that thou shouldst not assist me in obtaining this, which is so pleasing to thee? No; thou wilt assuredly help me, and pray for me. Pray, and cease not to pray, until thou seest me in paradise, safe from all danger of again losing my Lord, and secure of ever loving him, together with thee, my most dear mother.

SATURDAY

To Obtain the Patronage of Mary

O Most Holy Mother! I am sensible of the graces which thou hast obtained for me, and of the ingratitude with which I have employed them; but notwithstanding this, I will not cease to confide in thy mercy, which is much greater than my ingratitude. O my powerful advocate, have pity on me. Thou art the dispenser of all the graces which God grants to us miserable sinners. For this end has he made thee so powerful, so rich, and so benign, that thou mayest succor us in our miseries. O Mother of mercy, leave me not in my poverty. Thou art the advocate of the most miserable and abandoned sinners when they have recourse to thee; defend me, therefore, who recommend myself to thee. Say not that my cause is difficult to be gained; whilst the most desperate causes, when entrusted to thee, are always successful. In thy hands, therefore, do I place my eternal salvation, and to thee do I consign my soul, which was lost, but which thou wilt save by thy holy intercession. This is my hope. Amen.

CHAPTER III

THE PRACTICE OF THE CHRISTIAN VIRTUES

§ 1. The Practice of Humility

No one can please God without being humble, for he cannot bear the proud. He has promised to hear those who pray to him; but if a proud man prays to him, the Lord hears him not; to the humble, on the contrary, he dispenses his graces: *God resisteth the proud, and giveth grace to the humble.*[1]

Humility is of two kinds; humility of *affection*, and humility of the *will*. The former consists in the conviction we have of our own wretchedness, so that we can neither know nor do anything but what is evil. All that we have and do that is good comes from God. Let us come now to the practice of humility. With regard, then, to the humility of the affections, first, we must put no confidence in our own strength, nor in our own resolutions; but we must be always diffident and fearful of ourselves: *With fear and trembling work out your salvation.*[2] St. Philip Neri said: "He who fears not is sure to fall." Secondly; we must not glory in things that belong to us, as in our natural abilities, in our actions, in our birth, in our relatives, and the like. It is therefore well never to speak of our actions, except to point out where we have been wrong.

---

[1] "Deus superbis resistit; humilibus autem dat gratiam." – James iv. 6.
[2] "Cum metu et tremore vestram salutem operamini." – Phil. ii. 12.

And it is better not to speak of ourselves at all, either for good or bad; because, even when we blame ourselves, it is often an occasion of vain-glory, by making us think that we shall be praised, or at least be considered humble, and thus humility becomes pride. Thirdly, let us not be angry with ourselves after we have committed a fault. That would not be humility, but pride; and it is even a device of the devil to take away all our confidence, and make us leave off following a good life. When we see that we have fallen, we should say with St. Catharine of Genoa: "Lord, these are the fruits of my own garden." Then let us humble ourselves, and rise up immediately from the fault we have committed by an act of love and contrition, resolving not to fall into the same fault again, and trusting in the help of God. And if we unhappily do fall again, we must always do the same. Fourthly, when we see others fall, we are not to wonder; rather let us compassionate them; and let us thank God, praying him to keep his hand over us; otherwise the Lord will punish us by permitting us to fall into the same sins, and perhaps worse. Fifthly, we must always consider ourselves as the greatest sinners in the world; even when we know that others have sinned more than we; because our sins having been committed after we had received so many favors, and had been enlightened by so many graces, will be more displeasing to God than the faults of others, though they may be more numerous. St. Teresa writes that we must not think we have made any progress in the way of perfection if we do not esteem ourselves worse than every one else, and desire to be considered the last of all.

The humility of the *will* consists in being pleased when we are despised by others. Any one who has deserved hell, deserves to be trodden under foot by the devils forever. Jesus Christ desires that we should learn of him to be meek and humble of heart: *Learn of Me, because I am meek and humble of heart.*[3] Many are humble in word, but not in heart. They say: "I am worse than all: I deserve a thousand hells." But when

---

[3] "Discite a me, quia mitis sum et humilis corde." – Matt. xi. 29.

any one reproves them, or says a word that displeases them, they immediately take umbrage. They are like hedgehogs, which put out their bristles as soon as they are touched. But how is it – you say you are worse than all, and yet you cannot bear a word? "He who is truly humble," says St. Bernard, "esteems himself good for nothing, and desires to be considered good for nothing by others as well."

In the first place, then, if you wish to be truly humble, when you receive an admonition, receive it in good part, and thank the person who admonishes you. St. Chrysostom says, "When the just man is corrected, he is sorry for the error he has committed; but the proud man is sorry that the error should be known." The saints, when they are accused, even wrongfully, do not justify themselves, except when to defend themselves is necessary to avoid giving scandal: otherwise they are silent, and offer all to God.

In the second place, when you receive any affront, suffer it patiently, and increase in love towards the person who has ill-treated you. This is the touchstone by which you may know whether a person is humble and holy. If he resents an injury, even though he may work miracles, you may say that he is an empty reed. Father Balthazar Alvarez said that the time of humiliation is the time to gain treasures of merits. You will gain more by peaceably suffering contempt, than you could do by fasting ten days on bread and water. Humiliations which we inflict on ourselves are good; but those which we accept from the hands of others are worth much more, because in these last there is less of self and more of God; therefore, when we know how to bear them the merit is greater. But what can a Christian pretend to do if he cannot bear to be despised for the sake of God? How much contempt did not Jesus Christ suffer for us! Buffetings, derisions, scourging, and spitting in his face! Ah! if we loved Jesus Christ, not only should we not show resentment for injuries, but we should rejoice at seeing ourselves despised as Jesus Christ was despised.

§ 2. The Practice of Mortification

If any man will come after Me, let him deny himself, and take up his cross, and follow Me.[1] This is all that any one who wishes to be a follower of Jesus Christ has to do. The denying of one's self is the mortification of self-love. Do we wish to be saved? We must then conquer all to make sure of all. How miserable is the soul that allows itself to be guided by self-love! Mortification is of two kinds – *internal* and *external*: by interior mortification we have to study to conquer our passions, and especially our most predominant one. A person who does not overcome his predominant passion is in great danger of being lost; whereas he who has overcome that will easily conquer all the others. Some, however, allow one vice to predominate in themselves, and think that they are good, because they do not see in themselves vices which others have. "But what does it matter?" says St. Cyril: "one leak is sufficient to sink the ship." Nor will it suffice to say, "I cannot abstain from this vice;" a resolute will conquers all; that is, of course, with the assistance of God, who will never fail us.

---

[1] "Si quis vult post me venire, abneget semetipsum, et tollat crucem suam, et sequatur me." – Matt. xvi. 24.

External mortification has to do with conquering the sensual appetites. Worldly people call the saints cruel when they deny their bodies all satisfaction of the senses and chastise them with hair-shirts, disciplines, and other penances. "But," says St. Bernard, "they are in reality much more cruel to themselves, who condemn themselves to burn forever in hell-fire for the sake of the short and miserable pleasures of this life." Others say that all forbidden pleasures should be denied to the body; but they despise external mortifications, saying, that interior mortification is what is required; that is, the mortification of the will. Yes, it is principally necessary to mortify the will, but the mortification of the flesh is also necessary; because, when the flesh is not mortified, it will be hard to be obedient to God. St. John of the Cross said, that any one who taught that external mortification was not necessary, ought not to be believed, even though he worked miracles. But let us come to the practice of it.

In the first place, the eyes must be mortified. The first arrows which wound the soul, and often kill it, enter through the eyes. The eyes are, as it were, grappling-irons of hell, which drag souls, as if by main force, into sin. A certain Pagan philosopher voluntarily put out his eyes to free himself from impurity. It is not lawful for us to pluck out our eyes, but we ought to make them blind by means of mortification; otherwise we shall find it difficult to keep ourselves chaste. St. Francis de Sales said: "You must close the gates, if you do not wish the enemy to enter into the citadel." We must then abstain from looking at any object that may give occasion to temptation. St. Aloysius Gonzaga did not dare to raise his eyes to look even at his own mother; and when by chance our eyes light on some dangerous object, let us take care not to fix them on it. "It is not so much the mere seeing," says St. Francis de Sales, "but the inspecting and continuing to look, that is the cause of ruin." Let us then be very careful in mortifying our eyes; because many are now in hell on account of sins committed with the eyes.

In the second place, we must mortify our tongue, by abstaining from words of detraction, or of abuse, or of obscenity. An impure word spoken in conversation, even in jest, may prove a scandal to others, and be the cause of a thousand sins arising from it. And it should be observed, that sometimes a word of double meaning, said in a witty way, does more harm than a word openly impure.

In the third place, we must mortify the taste. St. Andrew Avellini said that, in order to begin to live a good Christian life, a man must begin by the mortification of his palate. And St. Francis de Sales said: "We must eat to live, not live to eat." Many seem to live only to eat, and thus they destroy the health both of their soul and body. For the most part costiveness, diarrhea, and other illnesses are caused by the vice of gluttony. But the worst is, that intemperance in eating and drinking is often the cause of incontinence. Cassian writes that it is impossible that a man who is satiated with food and heating drinks – as wine, brandy, and the like – should not feel many impure temptations. "But how is this?" says such a one; "must I eat no more?" Yes, my good friend, we must eat to preserve our life, but like rational beings, not as brutes. Especially if you desire to be free from impure temptations, abstain from eating overmuch meat, and from overmuch wine. The Scripture says: *Give not wine to kings.*[2] By a king is meant one who brings his flesh under the dominion of reason. Much wine makes us lose our reason, and involves not only the vice of drunkenness, which is certainly a mortal sin, but also that of impurity. Regret not having sometimes to fast or to abstain, especially on a Saturday, in honor of the Most Holy Mary. Many do so on bread and water; this you can at least do on the vigils of the seven principal feasts of Our Lady. I pray you to observe at least the fasts of obligation. Some go beyond fifteen or twenty ounces at collation, and say: "It is sufficient if I am not satisfied." No, it is not enough; the most that can be taken on the evenings of fast days of obligation is eight ounces; and

---

[2] "Noli regibus dare vinum." – Prov. xxxi. 4.

even that has grown up by custom; for in olden times food could be taken only once a day.

In the fourth place, we must mortify our hearing and our touch: the hearing, by avoiding listening to immodest and scandalous conversations; the touch, by using all possible caution, as well in regard to others as in regard to ourselves. Some say it is nothing, that they only do it in jest; but who, I ask, would play with fire?

§ 3. The Practice of Charity Towards our Neighbor

He who loves God, loves his neighbor also; but he who loves not his neighbor, neither does he love God; for the divine precept says, *That he who loveth God, loves also his brother*.[1] We must also love our neighbor in heart as well as in deed. And how much are we to love him? Here is the rule: *Love the Lord thy God with thy whole soul,... and thy neighbor as thyself*.[2] We must, then, love God above all things and more than ourselves; and our neighbor as ourselves. So that, as we desire our own good, and take delight in it when we have it, and, on the contrary, are sorry for any evil that may happen to us, so also we must desire our neighbor's good, and rejoice when he obtains it; and, on the other hand, we must be sorry for his misfortunes. So, again, we must neither judge nor suspect evil of our neighbor, without good grounds. And this is what constitutes interior charity.

External charity consists in our words and actions towards our neighbor. As to words, first we must abstain

---

[1] "Qui diligit Deum, diligat et fratrem suum." – John iv. 2.
[2] "Diliges Dominum Deum tuum ex toto corde tuo:...et proximum tuum sicut teipsum." – Luke x. 27.

from the least shadow of detraction. A detractor is hateful to God and man. On the contrary, he who speaks well of every one is beloved by God and men; and when the fault cannot be excused, we must at least excuse the intention. Secondly, let us be careful not to repeat to any one the evil that has been said of him by another; because sometimes long enmities and revenge arise from such things. The Scripture says, he who sows discord is hated by God. Thirdly, we must take care not to wound our neighbor, by saying anything that may hurt him; even were it only in jest. Would you like to be laughed at in the same way as you laugh at your neighbor? Fourthly, let us avoid disputes: sometimes, on account of a mere trifle, quarrels are begun which end in abuse and rancor. We have also to guard against the spirit of contradiction, which some indulge when they gratuitously set themselves to contradict everything. On such occasions give your opinion, and then be quiet. Fifthly, let us speak gently to all, even to our inferiors; therefore let us not make use of imprecations or abuse. And when our neighbor is angry with us, and is somewhat abusive, let us answer meekly, and the quarrel will be at an end: *A mild answer breaketh wrath.*[3] And when we are annoyed by our neighbor, we must be careful not to say anything; because our passion will then make us go too far: it will make us exaggerate; but afterwards we shall certainly be sorry for it. St. Francis de Sales says, "I was never angry in my life, that I did not repent of it shortly afterwards." The rule is to be silent as long as we feel ourselves disturbed. And when our neighbor continues to be irritated, let us reserve the correction till another time, even though it should be necessary; because for the moment our words would not convince, and would do no good.

With regard also to the charity of our actions towards our neighbor: first, it is practised by aiding him as we best may. Let us remember what the Scripture says: *For alms deliver from all sin and from death, and will not suffer the soul to*

---

[3] "Responsio mollis frangit iram." – Prov. xv. i.

go into darkness.[4] Almsgiving, then, saves us from sin and from hell. By alms is understood any assistance which it is in our power to render to our neighbor. The kind of almsgiving which is the most meritorious is to help the soul of our neighbor, by correcting him gently and opportunely, whenever we can. And let not us say with some, "What doth it signify to me?" It does signify to one who is a Christian. He who loves God, wishes to see him loved by all.

Secondly, we must show charity towards the sick, who are in greater need of help. Let us make them some little present, if they are poor. At least let us go: and wait on them and comfort them, even though they should not thank us for doing so; the Lord will reward us.

Thirdly, we must above all show charity to our enemies. Some are all kindness with their friends; but Jesus Christ says, *Do good to those that hate you.*[5] By this you may know that a man is a true Christian, if he seeks to do good to those who wish him evil. And if we can do nothing else for those who persecute us, let us at least pray that God will prosper them, according as Jesus commands us: *Pray for them that persecute you.*[6] This is the way the saints revenged themselves. He who pardons any one who has offended him, is sure of being pardoned by God; since God has given us the promise: *Forgive, and you shall be forgiven.*[7] Our Lord said one day to the Blessed Angela of Foligno, that the surest sign of a soul being loved by God, is when it loves a person who has offended it.

Fourthly, let us also be charitable to our neighbors who are dead, that is, to the holy souls in purgatory. St. Thomas says, that if we are bound to help our neighbors who are alive, we are also bound to remember them when dead. Those holy prisoners are suffering pains which exceed all the sufferings of this life; and nevertheless are in the greatest necessity,

---

[4] "Eleemosyna ab omni peccato et a morte liberat, et non patietur animam ire in tenebras." – Tob. iv. ii.
[5] "Benefacite his qui oderunt vos." – Matt. v. 44.
[6] "Orate pro persequentibus et calumniantibus vos." – Matt. v. 44.
[7] "Dimittite, et dimittemini." – Luke vi. 37.

since they cannot possibly help themselves. A Cistercian monk once said to the sacristan of his monastery: "Help me, brother, by your prayers, when I can no longer help myself." Let us then endeavor to succor these holy souls, either by having Masses said for them, or by hearing Masses for them, by giving alms, or at least by praying, and applying indulgences in their behalf; they will show themselves grateful by obtaining great graces for us, not only when they reach heaven, if they arrive there sooner through our prayers, but also in purgatory.

§ 4. The Practice of Patience

St. James says that patience is the perfect work of a soul; *And patience hath a perfect work.*[1] It is by patience that we gain heaven. This earth is a place where we can gain merit; therefore it is not a place of rest, but of labors and sufferings; and it is for this end that God makes us live here, that by patience we may obtain the glory of paradise. Every one has to suffer in this world; but he who suffers with patience suffers less and saves himself, while he who suffers with impatience suffers more and is damned. Our Lord does not send us crosses that he may see us lost, as some impatient people say, but that we may be thereby saved, and inherit more glory in heaven. Sorrows, contradictions, and all other tribulations, when accepted with patience, become the brightest jewels in our heavenly crown. Whenever, then, we are in affliction, let us console ourselves and thank God for it, since it is a sign that God wishes us to be saved, by chastising us in this life, where the chastisements are but slight and short, so as not to punish us in the next, where the chastisements are cruel and eternal. Woe to the sinner who

---

[1] "Patientia autem opus perfectum habet." – James i. 4.

is prosperous in this life! it is a sign that God has reserved for him eternal punishment.

St. Mary Magdalene of Pazzi said: "All sufferings, however great, become sweet when we look at Jesus on the cross." And St. Joseph Calasanctius: "He who cannot suffer for Jesus Christ, does not know how to gain Jesus Christ for his own." He, then, who loves Jesus Christ bears patiently all external crosses – sickness, pains, dishonor, loss of parents and friends; and all interior crosses – afflictions, weariness, temptations, and desolation of spirit, and he bears them all in peace. On the other hand, he who is impatient and angry when he is in tribulation, what does he do? He does but increase his suffering, and adds to his punishments in the next life. St. Teresa says in her writings: "The cross is felt by those who drag it after them by force; but he who embraces it with a good will does not feel it." Hence St. Philip Neri also said: "In this world there is no purgatory; it is either heaven or hell: he who bears tribulation with patience is in heaven, but he who does not, is in hell." Let us proceed to the practice.

First, patience must be practised in sickness. The time of sickness is a time for testing the devotion of people, whether it is of lead or of gold. Some are pious and cheerful when they are in good health; but when they are visited by any illness, they lose their patience, complain of everything, and give themselves up to melancholy, and commit a thousand other faults. Their gold turns out to be lead. St. Joseph Calasanctius said: "If sick people were patient, we should hear no more complaints." Some complain and say: "But as long as I am in this state, I cannot go to church, nor to Communion, nor to Mass; in short, I can do nothing." You say you can do nothing. You do everything when you do the will of God. Tell me, why do you want to do those things you have named? Is it to please God? This is the good pleasure of God, that you should embrace with patience all you have to endure, and should leave everything else that you wish to do alone. "God is served," writes St. Francis de Sales, "more by suffering than by any other works we can do."

If our sickness be dangerous, then especially must we accept it with all patience, being willing to die should the end of our life be really at hand. Nor should we say: "But I am not now prepared; I should like to live a little longer to do penance for my sins." And how do you know that if you were to live on you would do penance, and would not fall into greater sins? How many there are who, after recovering from some mortal illness, have become worse than they were before, and have been lost; while, perhaps, if they had died then, they would have been saved! If it is the will of God that you should leave this world, unite yourself to his holy will, and thank him for allowing you the help of the holy Sacraments, and accept death with tranquility, abandoning yourself into the arms of his mercy. This compliance with the divine will, by accepting death, will be sufficient to insure your eternal salvation.

In the second place, we must accept also with patience the death of our relatives and friends. Some on the death of a relative are so inconsolable, that they leave off saying their prayers, frequenting the sacraments, and all their devotions. Such a one goes so far as even to be angry with God, and to say: "Lord, why hast Thou done this?" What rashness is this! Tell me, what does all your grief profit you? Do you perhaps think to do pleasure to the dead person? No; what you are doing is displeasing to him as well as to God. He desires that, with regard to his death, you should become more united with God, and should pray for him if he is in purgatory.

In the third place, let us accept the poverty which God sends us. When you are in want even of the necessaries of life, say: "My God, Thou alone art sufficient for me." One such act will gain treasures for us in paradise. He who possesses God has every good. In the same way let us embrace with patience the loss of property, the failure of our expectations, or even the loss of those who were helping us. Let us be resigned at such times to the will of God, and God will help us; and if he should not then help us as we should wish, let us be content with whatever he may do, because he will do it to try our patience, that he may enrich us with greater merits and the goods of heaven.

In the fourth place, we must accept patiently contempt and persecutions. You will say: "But what evil have I done, that I should be so persecuted? Why have I had to suffer such an affront?" My brother, go and say this to Jesus Christ on the cross, and he will answer: "And I, what have I done, that I should have to suffer such sorrow and ignominy, and this death of the cross?" If, then, Jesus Christ has suffered so much for the love of you; it is no great thing that you should suffer this little for the love of Jesus Christ. Particularly if you have ever during your life committed some grievous sin, think that you deserve to be in hell, where you would have to suffer much greater contempt and persecution from the devils. If also you should be persecuted for having done good, rejoice exceedingly. Hear what Jesus Christ says: *Blessed are they that suffer persecution for justice' sake.*[2] Let us be convinced of the truth of what the Apostle says, that he who would live united with Jesus Christ in this world must be persecuted.

In the fifth place, we must practise patience also in spiritual desolations, which are the heaviest afflictions for a soul that loves God. But God in this way proves the love of his beloved ones. At such times let us humble ourselves and be resigned to the will of God, putting ourselves entirely into his hands. Let us be most careful also not to leave off any of our devotions, our prayers, frequenting of the sacraments, our visits to the Blessed Sacrament, or our spiritual reading. As we do everything then with weariness and trouble, it seems to us to be all lost, but it is not so: while we persevere in all these things, we work without any satisfaction to ourselves; but it is very pleasing to God.

In the sixth and last place, we must practise patience in temptations. Some cowardly souls, when a temptation lasts a long time, are disheartened, and will sometimes even say: God, then, desires my damnation. No; God permits us to be tempted, not for our damnation, but for our advantage, that

---

[2] "Beati, qui persecutionem patiuntur propter justitiam." – Matt. v. 10.

we may then humble ourselves the more, and unite ourselves more closely to him, by forcing ourselves to resist, redoubling our prayers, and thereby acquiring greater merits for heaven. *And because thou wast acceptable to God, it was necessary that temptation should prove thee.*³ Thus was it said to Tobias. Every temptation which we overcome gains for us fresh degrees of glory, and greater strength to resist future temptations. Nor does God ever permit us to be tempted beyond our strength: *And God is faithful, who will not suffer you to be tempted above what you are able; but will make also with temptation issue, that you may be able to bear it.*⁴

We should, however, beg our Lord to deliver us from temptations; notwithstanding, when they come, let us resign ourselves to his holy will, beseeching him to give us strength to resist. St. Paul was troubled with carnal temptations, and he prayed to God to deliver him from them; but the Lord said to him: *My grace is sufficient for thee; for power is made perfect in infirmity.*⁵ In sensual temptations especially the first precaution to be taken is to remove ourselves as far as possible from all occasions, and then immediately to have recourse to Jesus Christ for help, not trusting in our own strength. And when the temptation continues, let us not cease to pray, saying: "Jesus, help me! Mary, ever Virgin, assist me!" The mere invocation of these all-powerful names of Jesus and Mary will suffice to defeat the most violent assaults of hell. It is also of great use to make the sign of the cross on our forehead, or over our heart. By the sign of the cross, St. Anthony Abbot overcame similar attacks of the devil. It is also a very good thing to acquaint your spiritual father with your temptations. St. Philip Neri used to say: "A temptation which is manifested is half overcome."

---

³ "Quia acceptus eras Deo, necesse fuit ut tentatio probaret te." – Tob. xii 13.
⁴ "Fidelis autem Deus est, qui non patietur vos tentari supra id quod potestis: sed faciet etiam cum tentatione proventum." – I Cor. x. 13.
⁵ "Sufficit tibi, Paule, gratia mea; nam virtus in infirmitate perficitur." – 2 Cor. xii. 9.

§ 5. The Practice of Conformity to the Will of God

All sanctity consists in loving God; and the love of God consists in fulfilling his holy will. In this is our life: *And life in His good will.*[1] And he who is always united with the will of God is always in peace; for the divine will takes away the bitterness of every cross. By saying, *God wills it so, God has so willed,* holy souls find peace in all their labors: *Whatsoever shall befall the just man, it shall not make him sad.*[2] You say: 'Everything goes wrong with me; God sends me all kinds of misfortunes.' Things go wrong with you, my friend, because you make them go wrong; if you were to be resigned to the will of God, all would go well, and for your good. The crosses which God sends you are misfortunes, because you make them misfortunes; if you would take them with resignation, they would no longer be misfortunes, but riches for paradise. Ven. Balthazar Alvarez says: "He who in his troubles resigns himself with peacefulness to the divine will, runs to God post-haste." Let us now come to the practice.

---

[1] "Et vita in voluntate ejus." – Ps. xxix. 6.
[2] "Non contristabat justum, quidquid ei acciderit." – Prov. xii. 21.

And first, let us resign ourselves in the sicknesses which befall us. Worldly people call illnesses misfortunes, but the saints call them visitations of God and favors. When we are ill we ought certainly to take remedies in order to be cured, but we should always be resigned to whatever God disposes. And if we pray for restoration to health, let it always be done with resignation, otherwise we shall not obtain the favor. But how much do we not gain when we are ill by offering to God all we suffer! He who loves God from his heart does not desire to be cured of his illness in order not to suffer, but he desires to please God by suffering. It was this love which made the scourge, the rack, and the burning pitch sweet to the holy martyrs. We must also be especially resigned in mortal sickness. To accept death at such a time, in order that the will of God may be fulfilled, merits for us a reward similar to that of the martyrs, because they accepted death to please God. He who dies in union with the will of God makes a holy death; and the more closely he is united to it, the more holy death does he die. The Venerable Blosius declares that an act of perfect conformity to the will of God at the hour of death not only delivers us from hell, but also from purgatory.

Secondly, we must also unite ourselves to the will of God with regard to our natural defects, as want of talents, being of low birth, weak health, bad sight, want of ability for affairs, and the like. All that we have is the free gift of God. Might he not have made us a fly or a blade of grass? A hundred years ago were we anything but nothingness? And what more do we want? Let it suffice that God has given us the power of becoming saints. Although we may have little talent, poor health, and may be poor and abject, we may very well become saints through his grace if we have the will. Oh, how many unfortunate beings have been damned on account of their talents, their health, high birth, riches or beauty! Let us then be content with what God has done for us; and let us thank him always for the good things he has given us, and particularly for having called us to the holy faith; this is a great gift, and one for which few are found to thank God.

Thirdly, we must resign ourselves in all adversities that may happen to us, as the loss of property, of our expectations, of our relatives; and in the attacks and persecutions we may meet with from men. You will say: But God does not will sin; how is it that I must resign myself when some one calumniates me, wrongs me, attacks and defrauds me? That cannot happen by the will of God. What a deception is this! God does not will the sin of such a one; he permits it: but, on the other hand, he does will the adversity which you suffer by means of this person. So that it is our Lord himself who sends you that cross, though it comes to you by means of your neighbor; therefore even in these cases you must embrace the cross as coming from God. Nor let us seek to find out a reason for such treatment. St. Teresa says: "If you are willing to bear only those crosses for which you see a reason, perfection is not for you."

Fourthly, we must be resigned in aridity of soul; if, when we say our prayers, make our Communions, visit the Blessed Sacrament, etc., all seems to weary and give us no comfort, let us be satisfied in knowing that we please God, and that the less satisfaction we feel ourselves in our devotions the more pleasure do we give him. At no time can we know better our own insufficiency and misery than in the time of aridity; and therefore let us humble ourselves in our prayers, and put ourselves with resignation into God's hands, and say: "Lord, I do not deserve consolations; I desire nothing but that Thou have pity on me; keep me in Thy grace, and do with me what Thou wilt." And so doing, we shall gain more in one day of desolation than in a month of tears and sensible devotion.

And generally speaking, this should be the continual tenor of our prayers, offering ourselves to God, that he may do with us as he pleases; saying to him in our prayers, our Communions, and in the visit: "My God, make me do Thy will." In doing the will of God we shall do everything. For this end let us accustom ourselves to have always on our lips the ejaculation: *Fiat voluntas tua*! "Thy will be done," even in the least things we do; for instance, if we snuff out a candle, break a glass, or stumble over something, let us always repeat; "May the will of God be done!" When we lose any of our possessions, or when one of our relatives dies, or anything else of the same sort happens to us, let us say: "O Lord, it is Thy will, it is my will also." And when we fear any temporal ill, let us say: "O Lord, I will whatever Thou willest." Thus we shall be very pleasing in the sight of God, and shall be always in peace.

§ 6. The Practice of Purity of Intention

Purity of intention consists in doing everything with the sole view of pleasing God. The good or bad intention with which an action is performed renders it good or bad before God. St. Mary Magdalene de Pazzi says: "God rewards actions according to the amount of purity of intention with which they are done." Let us examine the practice of it.

In the first place, in all our exercises (of devotion), let us seek God and not ourselves: if we seek our own satisfaction we cannot expect to receive any reward from God. And this holds good for all spiritual works. How many labor and exhaust themselves in preaching, hearing confessions, serving at the altar, and in doing other pious works; and because in these they seek themselves and not God, they lose all! When we seek neither approbation nor thanks from others for what we do, it is a sign that we work for God's sake: as also when we are not vexed at the good we undertake not succeeding; or when we rejoice as much at any good that is done by others, as if it had been done by ourselves. Further, whenever we have done some good in order to please God, let us not torment ourselves in endeavoring to drive away vain-glory; if we are praised for it, it is enough to say: "To God be the honor and glory." And let us never omit doing any good action which may be edifying to our neighbor, through fear of vain-glory. Our Lord wishes us to do good even before others, that it may be profitable to them: *So let your light shine before men, that they may see your good works, and glorify your Father who is in heaven.*[1] Therefore when you do good, have first the intention of pleasing God; and secondly, that also of giving a good example to your neighbor.

In the second place, in our bodily actions; whether we work, eat, drink, or amuse ourselves with propriety, let us do all in order to please God. Purity of intention may be called the heavenly alchemy, which changes iron into gold; by which is meant, that the most trivial and ordinary actions when done to please God become acts of divine love. St. Mary Magdalene de Pazzi used to say: "A person who performs all his actions with a pure intention will go straight to paradise." A holy hermit, before putting his hand to any work, used to raise his eyes to heaven, and keep them fixed there for a short time; and when he was asked what he was doing, he answered; "I am taking my aim, so that I may not miss the mark." Let us also do in like manner: before beginning any action, let us make sure of our aim, and say: "Lord, I do this to please Thee."

---

[1] "Sic luceat lux vestra coram hominibus, ut videant opera vestra bona, et glorificent Patrem vestrum." – Matt. v. 16.

§ 7. Rules for Avoiding Tepidity

Souls that make no account of venial sins, and give themselves up to tepidity, without a thought of freeing themselves from it, live in great danger. We do not here speak of those venial sins that are committed by mere frailty, such as useless or idle words, interior disquietudes, and negligence in small matters; but we speak of venial sins committed with full deliberation, above all when they are habitual. St. Teresa writes thus: "From all deliberate sin, howsoever small it may be, O Lord, deliver us!" Ven. Alvarez used to say: "Those little backbitings, dislikes, culpable curiosity, acts of impatience and intemperance, do not indeed kill the soul, but they so weaken it, that when any great temptation takes it unexpectedly, it will not have strength enough to resist, and will consequently fall." So that as on the one hand deliberate venial sins weaken the soul, so on the other do they deprive us of the divine assistance; for it is but just that God should be sparing with those who are sparing towards him: *He who soweth sparingly, shall also reap sparingly.*[1] And that is what a soul that has received special graces from God has the most reason to fear. Still more ought it to fear

---

[1] "Qui parce seminat, parce et metet." – 2 Cor. ix. 6.

lest such faults should be caused by some passionate attachment, as of ambition, or avarice, or of aversion, or inordinate affection towards any person. It happens not infrequently to souls that are in bondage to some passion, as it does to gamblers, who, after losing many times, at the last throw say, "Let us risk everything;" and so finish by losing all they have. In what a miserable state is that soul which is the slave of some passion; for passion blinds us, and lets us no longer see what we are doing. Let us now come to the practice of what we have to do, in order to be able to deliver ourselves from the wretched state of tepidity.

It is necessary in the first place to have a firm desire to get out of this state. The good desire lightens our labor, and gives us strength to go forward. And let us rest assured that he who makes no progress in the way of God will always be going back; and he will go back so far that at last he will fall over some precipice. Secondly, let us try to find out our predominant faults to which we are most attached, whether it be anger, ambition, or inordinate affection to persons or things: a resolute will overcomes all with the help of God. Thirdly, we must avoid the occasion, otherwise all our resolutions will fall to the ground. And lastly, we must above all be diffident of our own strength, and pray continually with all confidence to God, begging him to help us in the danger in which we are, and to deliver us from those temptations by which we shall fall into sin; which is the meaning of the petition, *Ne nos inducas in tentationem* – "Lead us not into temptation." He who prays obtains: *Ask, and you shall receive.*[2] This is a promise of God, and can never fail; therefore we must always pray, always pray; and let us never leave off repeating, "We must pray always, we must pray always; my God help me, and that soon!"

---

[2] "Petite, et accipietis." – John xvi. 24.

§ 8. The Practice of Devotion Towards the Great Mother of God

As regards this devotion, I hope that the reader is fully persuaded that, in order to insure eternal salvation, it is most important to be devout to the Most Holy Mary. And if he should wish to be still more convinced of it, I would beg him to read the book I have written, called *The Glories of Mary*. We shall here speak only of the practices you may observe, that you may obtain the protection of this sovereign Lady.

First, every morning and evening, when you rise and before you go to bed, say three *Hail Marys*, adding this short prayer: "By thy pure and immaculate conception, O Mary, make me pure in body and holy in soul!" And put yourself beneath her mantle, that she may keep you that day or that night from sin. And every time you hear the clock strike, say a *Hail Mary*; do the same whenever you go in or out of the house, and when you pass by any picture or statue of the Blessed Virgin. So also when you begin and finish any of your occupations, such as your study, work, eating, or sleeping, never omit to say a *Hail Mary*. Secondly, say the Rosary, meditating on the mysteries, every day, at least five decades. Many devout people also say the Office of Our Lady; it would be well to say at least the Little Office of the Name of Mary, which is very short, and composed of five short psalms.

Thirdly, say an *Our Father* and *Hail Mary* every day to the ever-blessed Trinity in thanksgiving for the graces that have been bestowed upon Mary. The Blessed Virgin herself revealed to a person that this devotion was very pleasing to her. Fourthly, fast on bread and water every Saturday in honor of Mary, or at least on the vigils of her seven feasts; or at least fast in the ordinary way, or eat only of one dish, or abstain from something you like. In short, make use of some kind of mortification on Saturdays, and on the above-named vigils, for the sake of this Queen, who, as St. Andrew of Crete says, repays these little things with great graces. Fifthly, pay a visit every day to some image of your patroness, and ask her to give you holy perseverance and the love of Jesus Christ. Sixthly, let no day pass without reading a little about Our Lady, or else say some prayer to this Blessed Virgin. For this purpose we have here put seven prayers to Mary, for the seven days of the week (see Chap. II. § 7).

Seventhly, make the novenas for the seven principal feasts of Mary, and ask your confessor to tell you what devotions and mortifications you should practise during those nine days: say at least nine *Hail Marys* and *Glory be to the Father*, and beg her each day of the novena to give you some special grace that you need. Lastly, often recommend yourself to this divine Mother during the day, and particularly in time of temptation, saying at such times, and often repeating with great affection, "Mary, help me! help me, my Mother!" And if you love Mary, try to promote devotion to this great Mother of God among your relatives, friends, and servants.

§ 9. On the Practice of Certain Means by Which We May Acquire the Love of Jesus Christ

Jesus Christ ought to be our whole love. He is worthy of it, both because he is a God of infinite goodness, and because he has loved us to such an excess, that he died for us. Oh, how great are our obligations to Jesus Christ! All the good we enjoy, all our inspirations, calls, pardons, helps, hopes, consolations, sweetnesses, and loving affections, come to us through Jesus Christ. Let us see by what means we are to acquire this love of Jesus Christ.

In the first place, we must desire to have this love of Jesus Christ, and we must, therefore, often ask him to give it us, especially in our prayers, in our Communions, and in the visit to the Blessed Sacrament. And this grace must also be sought for at the hands of the ever-blessed Mary, from our guardian angel and our holy patrons, that they may enable us to love Jesus Christ. St. Francis de Sales says that the grace of loving Jesus Christ contains all other graces in itself; because he who truly loves Jesus Christ cannot be wanting in any virtue.

In the second place, if we wish to acquire the love of Jesus Christ, we must detach our hearts from all earthly affections; divine love will find no place in a heart that is full of this world. St. Philip Neri used to say: "The love we give to creatures is all so much taken from God."

In the third place, we must often exercise ourselves, especially when we pray, in making acts of love to Jesus Christ. Acts of love are the fuel with which we keep alive the fire of holy charity. Let us make acts of love and complacency, saying: "My Jesus, I rejoice that Thou art infinitely happy, and that Thy eternal Father loves Thee as much as himself!" Of benevolence: "I wish, my Jesus, that all could know and love Thee!" Of predilection, as: "My Jesus, I love Thee more than all things! I love Thee more than myself!" Let us also often make acts of contrition, which are called acts of sorrowful love.

In the fourth place, if any one wishes to make sure of being inflamed with love towards Jesus Christ, let him often try to meditate on his Passion. It was revealed to a holy solitary, that no exercise was more efficacious in enkindling love, than the consideration of the sufferings and ignominy which Jesus Christ endured for love of us. I say, it is impossible that a soul, meditating often on the Passion of Christ, should be able to resist his love. It was for this that, although he could have saved us by one drop of his blood, nay even by a single prayer, he chose to suffer so much, and to shed all his blood, that he might attract all hearts to love him; therefore he who meditates on his Passion does what is very agreeable to him. Do you, then, often make your meditation on the Passion of our Lord Jesus Christ. Do so at least every Friday, the day on which he died for the love of us. For this purpose I have written many meditations on the Passion of our Lord Jesus Christ, especially the *Darts Of Fire* which speak of the love which Jesus Christ has borne us in the great work of our redemption.[1]

---

[1] These will be found in Volume IV. of the ascetical works. – ED. This treatise is included in the second part of this present book. – CDF

Darts of Fire

Meditations Composed, Beloved, and Used Daily by St. Alphonsus de Liguori

Also referred to as
PROOFS THAT JESUS CHRIST HAS GIVEN US OF HIS LOVE IN THE WORK OF REDEMPTION

by
St. Alphonsus de Liguori
Doctor of the Church

This classic work of St. Alphonsus is from the Ascetical Works, Volume Four:

*The Incarnation, Birth and Infancy of Jesus Christ;
Or, The Mysteries of the Faith.*

The Centenary Edition

Edited by
Rev. Eugene Grimm
Priest of the Congregation of the Most Holy Redeemer.

Originally published by Benziger Brothers, Printers of the Holy Apostolic See, 1887.

INTRODUCTION

"Darts of Fire"

From Rev. Eugene Grimm, the original editor of this work, we read the following:

"Saint Alphonsus Liguori himself set a high value on this little treatise. He recommends it in several places of his works, and we read in one of his spiritual letters (December 18, 1767) that he himself used it nearly every day. In it is to be found the expression of those sentiments with which the saintly author mostly loved to nourish himself, and by which he sanctified his soul. In this treatise are chiefly repeated, under every form, the most fervent acts of contrition and of love. 'They are irresistible darts that pierce the hardest hearts, and inflame divine love in the coldest souls.' These pious reflections may be especially used when we are in the presence of the Blessed Sacrament, in our Visits, before and after Holy Communion, during Holy Mass and other divine services, or when we meditate on the Passion of our Lord. This treatise, entitled Darts of Fire, was published by the holy author in 1767."

It is fitting to place this work alongside *A Christian's Rule of Life* since, as we read on page 25 of this present edition, it is one of four books that he recommends to his religious congregation for use during their meditations. As he says in the latter work, highlighting the importance of daily meditation, "He who makes his meditation every day can scarcely fall into sin."[1] Meditation, an essential element in mental prayer, may always be done with the aid of a book, St. Alphonsus notes.

Further, St. Alphonsus states that a most efficacious subject for meditation is the Passion of Our Lord. As he wrote, "If any one wishes to make sure of being inflamed with love towards Jesus Christ, let him often try to meditate on his Passion. It was revealed to a holy solitary that no exercise was more efficacious in enkindling love than the consideration of the sufferings and ignominy which Jesus Christ endured for love of us. I say, it is impossible that a soul, meditating often on the Passion of Christ, should be able to resist his love."[2] With this in mind, he added, "Do you, then, often make your meditation on the Passion of our Lord Jesus Christ. Do so at least every Friday, the day on which he died for the love of us. For this purpose I have written many meditations on the Passion of our Lord Jesus Christ, especially the *Darts Of Fire* which speak of the love which Jesus Christ has borne us in the great work of our redemption."[3]

In light of the Saint's own words, and to further aid the faithful who make use of *A Christian's Rule of Life*, it was thought to be good to include *Darts of Fire* in this publication. Further, it seems best to approach *Darts of Fire* by reading one meditation a day, rather than reading through them continuously in one sitting.

Charles D. Fraune

---

[1] See page 12.
[2] See page 84.
[3] See page 84.

DARTS OF FIRE

Or "Proofs that Jesus Christ has Given us of His Love in the Work of Redemption"

By
St. Alphonsus Liguori

To any one who considers the immense love which Jesus Christ has shown us in his life, and especially in his death, it is impossible not to be stirred up and excited to love a God who is so enamoured of our souls. St. Bonaventure calls the wounds of our Redeemer wounds which pierce the hardest hearts, and inflame divine love in the coldest souls.[1]

Therefore, in this short examination of the love of Jesus Christ, let us consider, according to the testimony of the divine Scriptures, how much our loving Redeemer has done to make us understand the love that he bears us, and to oblige us to love him.

---

[1] "Vulnera corda saxea vulnerantia et mentes congelatas inflammantia." – *Stim. div. am.* p. I, c. I.

I

Dilexit nos, et tradidit semetipsum pro nobis.

"He hath loved us, and hath delivered Himself for us."
– Ephes. v. 2.

God had conferred so many blessings on men, thereby to draw them to love him; but these ungrateful men not only did not love him, but they would not even acknowledge him as their Lord. Scarcely in one corner of the earth, in Judea, was he recognized as God by his chosen people; and by them he was more feared than loved. He, however, who wished to be more loved than feared by us, became man like us, chose a poor, suffering, and obscure life, and a painful and ignominious death; and why? To draw our hearts to himself. If Jesus Christ had not redeemed us, he would not have been less great or less happy than he has always been; but he determined to procure our salvation at the cost of many labors and sufferings, as if his happiness depended on ours. He might have redeemed us without suffering; but no, – he willed to free us from eternal death by his own death; and though he was able to save us in a thousand ways, he chose the most humiliating and painful way of dying on the cross of pure suffering, to purchase the love of us, ungrateful worms of the earth. And what indeed was the cause of his miserable birth and his most sorrowful death, if not the love he had for us?

Ah, my Jesus, may that love which made Thee die for me on Calvary destroy in me all earthly affections, and consume me in the fire which Thou art come to kindle on the earth. I curse a thousand times those shameful passions which cost Thee so much pain. I repent, my dear Redeemer, with all my heart for all the offences I have committed against Thee. For the future I will rather die than offend Thee; and I wish to do all that I can to please Thee. Thou hast spared nothing for my love; neither will I spare anything for Thy love. Thou hast loved me without reserve; I also without reserve will love Thee. I love Thee, my only good, my love, my all.

II

Sic Deus dilexit mundum, ut Filium suum unigenitunt daret.

"God so loved the world, as to give His only-begotten Son." John iii. 16

Oh, how much does that little word *so* mean! It means that we shall never be able to comprehend the extent of such a love as this which made a God send his Son to die, that lost man might be saved. And who would ever have been able to bestow on us this gift of infinite value but a God of infinite love?

I thank thee, O Eternal Father! for having given me Thy Son to be my Redeemer; and I thank Thee, O great Son of God, for having redeemed me with so much suffering and love. What would have become of me, after the many sins that I have committed against Thee, if Thou hadst not died for me? Ah, that I had died before I had offended Thee, my Saviour! Make me feel some of that detestation for my sins which Thou hadst while on earth and pardon me. But pardon is not sufficient for me, Thou dost merit my love; Thou hast loved me even to death, unto death will I also love Thee. I love Thee, O infinite goodness, with all my soul; I love Thee more than myself; in Thee alone will I place all my affections. Do thou help me; let me no longer live ungrateful to Thee, as I have done hitherto. Tell me what Thou wouldst have of me, for, by Thy grace, all, all will I do. Yes, my Jesus, I love Thee, my treasure, my life, my love, my all.

III

Negue per sanguinem hircorum aut vitulorum, sed per proprium sanguinem introivit semel in sancta, aeterna redemptione inventa.

"Neither by the blood of goats or of calves, but by His own blood, entered once into the Holies, having obtained eternal redemption."
Heb. ix. 12.

And of what worth would the blood of all goats or even of all men be, if they were sacrificed to obtain divine grace for us? It is only the blood of this Man-God which would merit for us pardon and eternal salvation. But if God himself had not devised this way to redeem us, as he did by dying to save us, who ever would have been able to think of it? His love alone designed it and executed it. Therefore holy Job did well to cry out to this God who loves man so much: *What is man, O Lord, that Thou dost so exalt him? why is Thy heart so intent upon loving him? what is man that Thou shouldst magnify him? or why dost Thou set Thy heart upon him?*[1] Ah, my Jesus, one heart is but little with which to love Thee; if I loved Thee even with the hearts of all men, it would be too little. What ingratitude, then, would it be if I were to divide my heart between Thee and creatures! No, my love, Thou wouldst have it all, and well dost Thou deserve it; I will give it all to

---

[1] "Quid est homo, quia magnificas eum? aut quid apponis erga eum cor tuum?" – Job vii. 17.

Thee. If I do not know how to give it Thee as I ought, take it Thyself, and grant that I may be able to say to Thee with truth, *God of my heart?*[2]

Ah, my Redeemer, by the merits of the abject and afflicted life that Thou hast willed to live for me, give me true humility, which will make me love contempt and an obscure life. May I lovingly embrace all infirmities, affronts, persecutions and interior sufferings, and all the crosses which may come to me from Thy hands. Let me love Thee, and dispose of me as Thou wilt. O loving heart of my Jesus! make me love Thee by discovering to me the immense good that Thou art. Make me all Thine before I die. I love Thee, my Jesus, who art worthy to be loved. I love Thee with all my heart, I love Thee with all my soul.

---

[2] "Deus cordis mei." – Ps. lxxii. 26.

IV

Benignitas et humanitas apparuit Salvatoris nostri Dei.

"The goodness and kindness of God our Saviour appeared."
Tit. iii. 4.

God has loved man from all eternity. *I have loved thee with an everlasting love.*[1] "But," says St. Bernard, "before the Incarnation of the Word the divine Power appeared in creating the world, and the divine Wisdom in governing it; but when the Son of God became man, then was made manifest the love which God had for men."[2] And, in fact, after seeing Jesus Christ go through so afflicted a life and so painful a death, we should be offering him an insult if we doubted the great love which he bears us. Yes, he does surely love us; and because he loves us, he wishes to be loved by us. *And Christ died for all, that they also who live may not now live to themselves, but for Him who died for them and rose again.*[3]

Ah, my Saviour, when shall I begin to understand the love which Thou hast had for me? Hitherto, instead of loving Thee, I have repaid Thee with offences and contempt of Thy graces, but since Thou art infinite in goodness I will not lose confidence. Thou hast promised to pardon him who repents;

---

[1] "In charitate perpetua dilexi te." — Jer. xxxi. 3.
[2] In Nat. Domini, s. I.
[3] "Pro omnibus mortuus est Christus, ut et qui vivunt, jam non sibi vivant, sed ei qui pro ipsis mortuus est et resurrexit." — 2 Cor. v. 15.

for Thy mercy's sake fulfil Thy promise to me. I have dishonored Thee by putting Thee aside to follow my own pleasures; but now I grieve for it from the bottom of my soul, and there is no sorrow that afflicts me more than the remembrance of having offended Thee, my Sovereign Good; pardon me and unite me entirely to Thee by an eternal bond of love, that I may not leave Thee any more, and that I may only live to love Thee and to obey Thee. Yes, my Jesus, for Thee alone will I live, Thee only will I love. Once I left Thee for creatures, now I leave all to give myself wholly to Thee. I love Thee, O God of my soul, I love Thee more than myself. O Mary, Mother of God, obtain for me the grace to be faithful to God till death.

V

In hoc apparuit charitas Dei in nobis, quoniam filium suum unigenitum misit Deus in mundum, ut vivamus per eum.

"By this hath the charity of God appeared toward us, because God hath sent His only-begotten Son into the world that we might live by Him."
I John iv. 9.

All men were dead by sin, and they would have remained dead if the eternal Father had not sent his Son to restore them to life by his death. But how? What is this? A God to die for man! A God! And who is this man? "Who am I?"[1] says St. Bonaventure. "O Lord, why hast Thou loved me so much?"[2] But it is in this that the infinite love of God shines forth. *By this hath the charity of God appeared.*[3] The Holy Church exclaims on Holy Saturday, "O wonderful condescension of Thy mercy toward us! O inestimable affection of charity! That Thou mightest redeem a slave, Thou didst deliver up Thy Son."[4] O immense compassion! O prodigy! O excess of the love of God? To deliver a servant and a sinner from the death that he deserves, his innocent Son is condemned to die.

---

[1] "Quid sum ego?"
[2] "Quare, Domine, cur me tam amasti?" — *Stim. div. am.* p. I, c. 13.
[3] "In hoc apparuit charitas Dei." — I John iv. 9
[4] "O mira circa nos tuae pietatis dignatio! O inaestimabilis dilectio charitatis; ut servum redimeres, Filium tradidisti!"

Thou, then, O my God, hast done this that we might live by Jesus Christ: *that we might live by Him.*[5] Yes, indeed, it is but meet that we should live for him, who has given all his blood and his life for us. My dear Redeemer, in the presence of Thy wounds and of the cross on which I see Thee dead for me, I consecrate to Thee my life and my whole will. Ah, make me all Thine, for from this day forward I seek and desire none but Thee. I love Thee, infinite Goodness; I love Thee, infinite Love; while I live may I always repeat, *My God, I love Thee, I love Thee*; let my last words in death be, *My God, I love Thee, I love Thee.*

---

[5] "Ut vivamus per eum." — I John iv. 9.

VI

Per viscera misericordiae Dei nostri, in quibus visitavit nos Oriens ex alto.

"Through the bowels of the mercy of our God, in which the Orient from on high hath visited us."
Luke i. 78.

Behold, the Son of God comes on earth to redeem us, and he comes stimulated alone by the bowels of his mercy. But, O God! if Thou hast compassion on lost man, is it not enough that Thou shouldst send an angel to redeem him? No, says the Eternal Word, I will come myself, that man may know how much I love him. St. Augustine writes: "For this reason chiefly did Jesus Christ come, that man should know how much God loves him."[1] But, my Jesus, even now that Thou hast come, how many men are there who truly love Thee? Wretch that I am, Thou knowest how I have hitherto loved Thee; Thou knowest what contempt I have had for Thy love. Oh that I might die of grief for it! I repent, my dear Redeemer, of having so despised Thee. Ah, pardon me, and at the same time give me grace to love Thee. Let me no longer remain unmindful of that great affection which Thou hast borne me. I love Thee now, but I love Thee but little. Thou dost merit an infinite love. Grant me at least that I may love Thee with

---

[1] "Maxime propterea Christus advenit, ut cognosceret homo quantum eum diligat Deus." — *De catech. rud.* c. 4.

all my strength. Ah, my Saviour, my joy, my life, my all, whom should I love if I love not Thee, the infinite Good? I consecrate all my wishes to Thy will; at the sight of the sufferings Thou hast undergone for me, I offer myself to suffer as much as it shall please Thee. *Lead us not into temptation, but deliver us from evil.*[2] Deliver me from sin, and then dispose of me as Thou wilt. I love Thee, infinite Good, and I am content to receive any punishment, even to be annihilated, rather than to live without loving Thee.

---

[2] "Ne nos inducas in tentationem, sed libera nos a malo."

VII

Et Verbum caro factum est.

"And the Word was made flesh."
John i. 14.

God sent the Archangel Gabriel to ask Mary's consent that he should become her Son; Mary gives her consent, and behold the Word is made man. O wonderful prodigy! at which the heavens and all nature stand in astonishment! The Word made flesh! A God made man! What if we were to see a king become a worm, to save the life of a little worm of earth by his death?

So, then, my Jesus, Thou art my God, and not being able to die as God, Thou hast been pleased to become man capable of dying in order to give Thy life for me. My sweet Redeemer, how is it that, at the sight of such mercy and love Thou hast shown towards me, I do not die of grief? Thou didst come down from heaven to seek me, a lost sheep; and how many times have I not driven Thee away, preferring my miserable pleasures before Thee! But since Thou dost wish to have me, I leave all; I wish to be Thine, and I will have none other but Thee. Thee do I choose for the only object of my affections. *My Beloved to me, and I to Him.*[1] Thou dost think of me, and I will think of none but Thee. Let me always love Thee, and

---

[1] "Dilectus meus mihi, et ego illi." — Cant. ii. 16.

may I never leave off loving Thee. Provided I can love Thee, I am content to be deprived of all sensible consolation, and even to suffer all torments. I see that Thou dost indeed wish me to be all Thine, and I wish to belong entirely to Thee. I know that every thing in the world is a falsehood, a deceit, nothing but smoke, filth, and vanity. Thou alone art the true and only good; therefore Thou alone art sufficient for me. *My God, I wish for Thee alone, and nothing else;* God hear me, *for Thee alone do I wish, and nothing else.*

VIII

Semetipsum exinanivit.

"He emptied Himself."
Phil. ii. 7.

Behold the only-begotten Son of God, omnipotent and true God, equal to the Father, born a little Infant in a stable. *He emptied Himself, taking the form of a servant, being made to the likeness of men.*[1] If any one would see a God annihilated, let him enter into the cave of Bethlehem, and he will find him as a little Infant, bound in swaddling-clothes, so that he cannot move, weeping and trembling with cold. Ah, holy faith, tell me whose Son is this poor child? Faith answers, he is the Son of God, and he is true God. And who has brought him to so miserable a condition? It was the love he had for men. And yet there are men to be found who do not love this God!

Thou, then, my Jesus, hast spent all Thy life amidst sorrows to make me understand the love Thou dost bear me, and I have spent my life in despising and displeasing Thee by my sins! Ah, make me know the evil I have committed, and the love which Thou desirest to have. But since Thou hast borne with me till now, permit me not to give Thee any more cause for sorrow. Inflame me altogether with Thy love, and remind me always of all Thou hast suffered for me, that from

---

[1] "Semetipsum exinanivit, formam servi accipiens, in similitudinem hominum factus." — Phil. ii. 7.

this day forth I may forget everything, and think of nothing but loving and pleasing Thee. Thou didst come on earth to reign in our hearts; take, then, from my heart all that could prevent Thee from possessing it entirely! Make my will to be wholy conformed to Thy will; may Thine be mine, and may it be the rule of all my actions and desires.

IX

Parvulus natus est nobis, et Filius datus est nobis.

"For a child is born to us, and a Son is given to us."
Isa. ix. 6.

Behold the end for which the Son of God will be born an Infant, to give himself to us from his childhood, and thus to draw to himself our love. Why (writes St. Francis de Sales) does Jesus take the sweet and tender form of an Infant, if it be not to stimulate us to love him and to confide in him? St. Peter Chrysologus had said before, "Thus he willed to be born, because he wished to be loved."[1]

Oh, dear child Jesus, my Saviour! I love Thee, in Thee do I trust, Thou art all my hope and all my love. What would have become of me if Thou hadst not come down from heaven to save me? I know the hell which would have awaited me for the offences I have offered Thee. Blessed be Thy mercy, because Thou art ever ready to pardon me if I repent of my sins. Yes, I repent with all my heart, my Jesus, of having despised Thee. Receive me into Thy favor, and make me die to myself to live only to Thee, my only good. Destroy in me, O thou consuming fire, everything that is displeasing in Thine eyes, and draw all my affections to Thee. I love Thee, O God of my soul, I love Thee, my treasure, my life, my all. I

---

[1] "Sic nasci voluit, qui voluit amari." — Serm. 158.

love Thee, and I wish to die saying, my God, I love Thee; and begin then to love Thee with a perfect love which shall have no end.

X

Rorate, caeli, desuper, et nubes pluant Justum. – Emitte Agnum, Domine, dominatorem terra. – Salutare tuum da nobis.

"Drop down dew, O ye heavens, from above, and let the clouds rain the just." – "Send forth the Lamb, the Ruler of the earth."
Isa. xlv. 8; xvi. i.

"Grant us Thy salvation."
Ps. lxxxiv. 8.

Thus did the holy Prophets desire for so many years the coming of the Saviour. The same prophet Isaias said: *Oh, that Thou wouldst send the heavens, and wouldst come down: the mountains would melt away at Thy presence, . . . the waters would burn with fire.*[1] Lord, he said, when men shall see that Thou hast come on earth out of love for them, the mountains shall be made smooth, that is, men in serving Thee will conquer all the difficulties that at first appeared to them insuperable obstacles. The waters would burn with fire, and the coldest hearts will feel themselves burning with Thy love, at the sight of Thee made man, and how well has this been verified in many happy souls! – in St. Teresa, in St. Philip Neri, St.

---

[1] "Utinam dirumperes coelos et descenderes; a facie tua monies defluerent…, aquae arderent igni." — Isa. lxiv. i, 2.

Francis Xavier, who even in this life were consumed by this holy fire. But how many such are there? Alas! but too few.

Ah, my Jesus, amongst these few I wish also to be. How many years ought I not already be burning in hell, separated from Thee, hating and cursing Thee forever. But no, Thou hast borne with me with so much patience, that Thou mightest see me burn, not with that unhappy flame, but with the blessed fire of Thy love; for this end Thou hast given me so many illuminations, and hast so often wounded my heart while I was far from Thee; finally, Thou hast done so much that Thou hast forced me to love Thee by Thy sweet attractions. Behold, I am now Thine. I will be Thine always and altogether. It remains for Thee to make me faithful, and this I confidently hope from Thy goodness. O my God! who could ever have the heart to leave Thee again and to live even a moment without Thy love? I love Thee, my Jesus, above all things; but this is little. I love Thee more than myself, but this is little also; I love Thee with all my heart, and this also is little. My Jesus, hear me, give me more love, more love, more love. O Mary, pray to God for me.

XI

Despectum, et novissintum virorum.

"Despised, and the most abject of men."
Isa. liii. 3.

Behold what was the life of the Son of God made man, the most abject of men. He was treated as the vilest, the least of men. To what extreme of meanness could the life of Christ be reduced greater than that of being born in a stable? of living as a servant in an unknown and despised shop? struck, treated as a mock king, having his face spit upon? and, finally, of dying condemned as a malefactor on an infamous gibbet?

St. Bernard exclaims, "Oh, lowest and highest!"[1] A God, Thou art the Lord of all, and how art Thou contented to be the most despised of all? And I, my Jesus, when I see Thee so humiliated for me, how can I wish to be esteemed and honored by all? A sinner to be proud! Ah, my despised Redeemer, may Thy example inspire me with love of contempt and of an obscure life; from this time forward I hope, with Thy help, to accept from my heart all opprobrium that I may have to suffer for the love of Thee, who hast endured so much for the love of me. Pardon me the pride of my past life, and give me love in its place. I love Thee, my despised Jesus. Go before me with Thy cross. I will follow

---

[1] "O novissimum et altissimum." — *S. de Passione.*

Thee with mine, and I will not leave Thee till I die crucified for Thee, as Thou didst die crucified for me. My Jesus, my despised Jesus, I embrace Thee; in Thy embrace will I live and die.

XII

Virum dolorum.

"A man of sorrows."
Isa. liii. 3.

What was the life of Jesus Christ? A life of sorrows; a life of internal and external sorrows from the beginning to the end. But what most afflicted Jesus Christ during the course of his life was the sight of the sins and the ingratitude with which men repaid the pains he had suffered with so much love for us. This thought had made him the most afflicted amongst all men that had ever lived on the earth.

So, then, my Jesus, I also added to the affliction Thou didst suffer during the whole of Thy life by my sins. And why do I not also say, as did St. Margaret of Cortona, who, when exhorted by her confessor to calm her grief and not to weep any more because God had pardoned her, redoubled her tears and answered, "Ah, my Father, how can I leave off weeping when I know that my sins afflicted my Jesus through the whole of his life?" Oh that I could die of grief, my Jesus, whenever I think of all the bitter anguish I have caused Thee every day of my life! Alas, how many nights have I slept deprived of Thy grace! How many times hast Thou pardoned me, and I have again turned my back upon Thee! My dear Lord, I repent above all things for having offended Thee. I love Thee with all my heart; I love Thee with all my soul.

"Ah, my sweet Jesus, permit me not to be separated any more from Thee."[1] Let me die rather than betray Thee afresh. O Mary, Mother of perseverance, obtain for me the gift of holy perseverance.

---

[1] "Jesu dulcissime! ne permittas me separari a te, ne permittas me separari a te."

XIII

Cum dilexisset suos, qui erant in mundo, in finem dilexit eos.

"Having loved his own who were in the world, He loved them unto the end."
John xiii. i.

    The love of friends increases at the time of death, when they are on the point of being separated from those they love; and it is then, therefore, that they try more than ever, by some pledge of affection, to show the love they bear to them. Jesus during the whole of his life gave us marks of his affection, but when he came near the hour of his death he wished to give us a special proof of his love. For what greater proof could this loving Lord show us than by giving his blood and his life for each of us? And not content with this, he left this very same body, sacrificed for us upon the cross, to be our food, so that each one who should receive it should be wholly united to him, and thus love should mutually increase.
    O infinite goodness! O infinite love! Ah, my enamoured Jesus, fill my heart with Thy love, so that I may forget the world and myself, to think of nothing but loving and pleasing Thee. I consecrate to Thee my body, my soul, my will, my liberty. Up to this time I have sought to gratify myself to Thy great displeasure; I am exceedingly sorry for it, my crucified love; hence forth I will seek nothing but Thee, *my God and my*

all.[1] My God, Thou art my all, I wish for Thee alone and nothing more. Oh that I could spend myself all for Thee, who hast spent Thyself all for me! I love Thee, my only good, my only love. I love Thee, and abandon myself entirely to Thy holy will. Make me love Thee, and then do with me what Thou wilt.

---

[1] "Deus meus et omnia."

XIV

Tristis est anima mea usque ad mortem.

"My soul is sorrowful even unto death."
Matt. xxvi. 38.

These were the words that proceeded from the sorrowful heart of Jesus Christ in the garden of Gethsemani, before he went to die. Alas, whence came this extreme grief of his, which was so great that it was enough to kill him? Perhaps it was on account of the torments that he saw he should have to suffer? No; for he had foreseen these torments from the time of his incarnation. He had foreseen them, and had accepted them of his own free will: *He was offered because it was His own will.*[1] His grief came from seeing the sins men would commit after his death. It was then, according to St. Bernardine of Sienna, that he saw clearly each particular sin of each one of us. He had regard to every individual sin.[2]

It was not, then, my Jesus, the sight of the scourges, of the thorns, and of the cross which so afflicted Thee in the garden of Gethsemani; it was the sight of my sins, each one of which so oppressed Thy heart with grief and sadness that it made Thee agonize and sweat blood. This is the recompense I have made Thee for the love Thou hast shown me by dying for me. Ah, let me share the grief Thou didst feel

---

[1] "Oblatus est, quia ipse voluit." — Isa. liii. 7.
[2] "Ad quamlibet culpam singularem habuit aspectum." — *T.* ii. s. 56, a. i.

in the garden for my sins, so that the remembrance of it may make me sad for all my life. Ah, my sweet Redeemer, if I could but console Thee as much now by my grief and love as I then afflicted Thee! I repent, my Love, with all my heart for having preferred my own miserable satisfaction to Thee. I am sorry, and I love Thee above all things. Although I have despised Thee, yet I hear Thee ask for my love. Thou wouldst have me love Thee with all my heart: *Love the Lord thy God with all thy heart, and with all thy soul.*[3] Yes, my God, I love Thee with all my heart, I love Thee with all my soul. Do Thou give me the love Thou requirest of me. If I have hitherto sought myself, I will now seek none but Thee. And seeing that Thou hast loved me more than others, more than others will I love Thee. Draw me always more, my Jesus, to Thy love by the odor of Thy ointments, which are the loving attractions of Thy grace. Finally, give me strength to correspond to so much love which God has borne to an ungrateful worm and traitor. Mary, Mother of mercy, help me by thy prayers.

---

[3] "Diliges Dominum Deum tuum ex toto corde tuo, et in tota anima tua." — Matt. xxii. 37.

XV

Comprehenderunt Jesum, et ligaverunt eum.

"They took Jesus and bound him."
John xviii. 12.

A God taken and bound! What could the angels have said at seeing their king with his hands bound, led between soldiers through the streets of Jerusalem! And what ought we to say at the sight of our God, who is content for our sake to be bound as a thief, to be presented to the judge who is to condemn him to death? St. Bernard laments, saying, "What hast Thou to do with chains?"[1] What have malefactors and chains to do with Thee, O my Jesus, Thou who art infinite goodness and majesty? They should belong to us sinners, guilty of hell, and not to Thee who art innocent and the Holy of holies. St. Bernard goes on to say, on seeing Jesus guilty of death, "What hast Thou done, my innocent Saviour, that Thou shouldst be thus condemned?"[2] O my dear Saviour, Thou art innocence itself; for what crime hast Thou been thus condemned? Ah, I will tell Thee, he replies: the crime Thou hast committed is the too great love Thou hast borne to men. Thy sin is love.[3]

---

[1] "Quid tibi et vinculis?" — *Lib. de Pass.* c. 4.
[2] "Quid fecisti, innocentissime Salvator, quod sic condemnareris?" — *Lib. de Pass.* c. 4.
[3] "Peccatum tuum amor tuus."

My beloved Jesus, I kiss the cords that bind Thee, for they have freed me from those eternal chains which I have deserved. Alas! how many times have I renounced Thy friendship and made myself a slave of Satan, dishonoring Thy infinite majesty! I grieve above all things for having so grievously insulted Thee. Ah, my God, bind my will to Thy feet with the sweet cords of Thy holy love, that it may wish for nothing but what is pleasing to Thee. May I take Thy will for the sole guide of my life. As Thou hast had so great care for my good, may I not care for anything but to love Thee. I love Thee, my sovereign Good; I love Thee, the only object of my affections. I know that Thou alone hast loved me truly, and Thee alone will I love. I renounce everything. Thou alone art sufficient for me.

XVI

Ipse autem vulneratus est propter iniquitates nostras, attritus est propter scelera nostra.

"But He was wounded for our iniquities, He was bruised for our sins."
Isa. liii. 5.

One single blow suffered by this Man-God was sufficient for the sins of the whole world; but Jesus Christ was not satisfied with that; he wished to be *wounded and bruised*[1] for our iniquities, which means to say, wounded and torn from head to foot, so that there should be no whole part remaining in his sacred body. Hence the same prophet beheld him full of sores like a leper. *And we have thought Him as it were a leper, and as one struck by God and afflicted.*[2]

O wounds of my sorrowful Jesus, you are all living evidences of the love which my Redeemer preserves for me; with tender words do you force me to love him for the many sufferings that he has undergone for the love of me. Ah, my sweet Jesus, when shall I give myself all to Thee, as Thou hast given Thyself all to me? I love Thee, my sovereign good. I love Thee, my God, lover of my soul. O God of love, give me love. By my love let me atone to Thee for the bitterness I

---

[1] "Vulneratus, attritus."
[2] "Et nos putavimus eum quasi leprosum, et percussum a Deo, et humiliatum." — Isa. liii. 4.

have given Thee in times past. Help me to drive from my heart everything that does not tend to Thy love.

Eternal Father, *look at the face of Thy Christ*,[3] look at the wounds of Thy Son, which seek pity for me, and for their sake pardon me the outrages that I have committed against Thee; take my heart entirely to Thyself, that it may not love, seek, nor sigh after any other but Thee. I say to Thee, with St. Ignatius, "Give me only love of Thee and Thy grace and I am rich enough."[4] Behold this is all I ask of Thee, O God of my soul; give me Thy love, together with Thy grace, and I desire nothing else. O Mary, Mother of God, intercede for me.

---

[3] "Respice in faciem Christi tui." — Ps. lxxxiii. 10.
[4] "Amorem tui solum cum gratia tua mihi dones, et dives sum satis."

XVII

Ave, Rex Judaorum.

"Hail, King of the Jews."
Matt. xxvii. 39.

Thus was our Redeemer scornfully saluted by the Roman soldiers. After having treated him as a false king, and having crowned him with thorns, they knelt before him and called him king of the Jews, and then, rising up with loud cries and laughter, they struck him and spit in his face. St. Matthew writes: *And platting a crown of thorns, they put it on His head...And bowing the knee before Him, they mocked Him, saying, Hail, King of the Jews; and spitting upon Him they took the reed and struck His head.* And St. John adds, *And they gave Him blows.*[1]

O my Jesus! this barbarous crown that encircles Thy head, this vile reed that Thou dost hold in Thy hand, this torn purple garment that covers Thee with ridicule, make Thee known indeed as a king, but a king of love. The Jews will not acknowledge Thee for their king, and they say to Pilate, *We have no King but Caesar.*[2] My beloved Redeemer, if

---

[1] "Et plectentes coronam de spinis, posuerunt super caput ejus, et arundinem in dextera ejus. Et genu flexo ante eum, illudebant ei dicentes: Ave, Rex Judaeorum. – Et expuentes in eum, acceperunt arundinem, et percutiebant caput ejus." – Matt, xxvii. 29. – "Et dabant ei alapas." — John xix. 3.

[2] "Non habemus regem, nisi Caesarem." — John xix. 15.

others will not have Thee for their king, I accept Thee, and desire that Thou shouldst be the only King of my soul. To Thee do I consecrate my whole self; dispose of me as Thou pleasest. For this end hast Thou endured contempt, so many sorrows, and death itself, to gain our hearts and to reign therein by Thy love. *For this end Christ died,…that he might be Lord both of the dead and of the living.*[3] Make Thyself, therefore, master of my heart, O my beloved King, and reign and exercise Thy sway there forever. Formerly I refused Thee for my Lord, that I might serve my passions; now I will be all Thine and Thee alone will I serve. Ah, bind me to Thee by Thy love, and make me always remember the bitter death that Thou hast willed to suffer for me. Ah, my King, my God, my love, my all, what do I wish for if not for Thee alone! – *Thee, God of my heart, and my portion forever.*[4] O God of my heart! I love Thee; Thou art my portion, Thou art my only good.

---

[3] "In hoc enim Christus mortuus est et resurrexit, ut et mortuorum et vivorum dominetur." — Rom. xiv. 9.
[4] "Deus cordis mei, et pars mea, Deus, in aeternum." — Ps. lxxii. 26.

XVIII

Et bajulans sibi crucem, exivit in cum, qui dicitur Calvariae, locum.

"And bearing His own Cross, He went forth to that place which is called Calvary."
John xix. 17.

Behold the Saviour of the world has now set out on his journey with his cross on his shoulders, going forth to die in torments for the love of men. The divine Lamb allows himself to be led without complaining, to be sacrificed upon the cross for our salvation. Go thou, also, my soul, accompany and follow thy Jesus, who goes to suffer death for thy love, to satisfy for thy sins. Tell me, my Jesus and my God, what dost Thou expect from men by giving Thy life for their sake? St. Bernard answers, Thou dost expect nothing but to be loved by them: "When God loves, he wishes for nothing but to be loved in return."[1]

Is it, then, my Redeemer, at so great a cost that Thou hast desired to gain our love? And shall there be any among men who believe in Thee, and not love Thee? I comfort myself with the thought that Thou art the love of all the souls of the saints, the love of Mary, the love of Thy Father; but, O my God, how many are there who will not know Thee, and

---

[1] "Cum amat Deus, non aliud vult, quam amari." — *In Cant.* s. 83.

how many that know Thee and yet will not love Thee! Infinite Love, make Thyself known, make Thyself loved. Ah, that I could by my blood and my death make Thee loved by all! But alas that I have lived so many years in the world while I knew Thee, but did not love Thee! But now at last Thou hast drawn me to love Thee by Thy so great goodness. At one time I was so unhappy as to lose Thy grace; but the grief I now feel for it, the desire of being all Thine, and still more the death Thou hast suffered for me, give me a firm confidence, O my Love, that Thou hast already pardoned me, and that now Thou dost love me. Oh that I could die for Thee, my Jesus, as Thou hast died for me! Although no punishment awaited those who love Thee not, I would never leave off loving Thee, and I would do all I could to please Thee. Thou who givest me this good desire, give me strength to follow it out. My love, my hope, do not abandon me; make me correspond, during the remainder of my life to the especial love that Thou has borne me. Thou desirest to have me for Thine own, and I wish to be all for Thee. I love Thee, my God, my treasure, my all. I will live and die always repeating, I love Thee, I love Thee, I love Thee.

XIX

Quasi agnus coram tondente se, obmutescet et non aperiet os suum.

"And shall be dumb as a lamb before his shearer, and He shall not open his mouth."
Is. liii. 7.

This was precisely the passage which the eunuch of Queen Candace was reading; but not understanding of whom it was written, St. Philip, inspired by God, entered the carriage in which the eunuch was, and explained to him that these words referred to our Redeemer Jesus Christ. Jesus was called a lamb because he was dragged into the praetorium of Pilate, and then led to death just like an innocent lamb. Therefore the Baptist calls him a lamb. *Behold the Lamb of God, behold Him who taketh away the sins of the world.*[1] A lamb who suffers and dies a victim on the cross for our sins. *Surely he hath borne our infirmities and carried our sorrows.*[2] Miserable are those who do not love Jesus Christ during their life. In the last day the sight of this Lamb in his wrath will make them say to the mountains, *Fall upon us and hide us from the*

---

[1] "Ecce Agnus Dei, ecce qui tollit peccata mundi." — John i. 29.
[2] "Vere languores nostros ipse tulit, et dolores nostros ipse portavit." — Isa. liii. 4.

face of Him that sitteth upon the throne, and from the wrath of the Lamb.[3]

No, my divine Lamb, if in times past I have not loved Thee, now I will love Thee forever. Before, I was blind; but now that thou hast enlightened me, and hast made me know the great evil I have done in turning my back upon Thee, and the infinite love which is due to Thee for Thy goodness and for the love Thou hast borne me, I repent with all my heart for having offended Thee, and I love Thee above all things. O wounds, O blood of my Redeemer, how many souls have you not inflamed with love! Inflame my soul also. Ah, my Jesus, continually call to my remembrance Thy Passion and the pains and ignominies that Thou hast suffered for me, that I may detach my affections from earthly goods and place them all on Thee, my only and infinite good.

I love Thee, Lamb of God, sacrificed and annihilated on the cross for my sake. Thou hast not refused to suffer for me; I will not refuse to suffer for Thee whatever Thou requirest. I will no longer complain of the crosses that Thou dost send me. I ought to have been in hell these many years; how, then, can I complain? Give me grace to love Thee, and then do with me what Thou wilt. *Who shall separate me from the love of Christ?*[4] Ah, my Jesus, sin alone can separate me from Thy love. Ah, let it not be; rather let me die a thousand times; this I beg of Thee by Thy sacred Passion. I beseech thee, O Mary, by thy sorrows deliver me from the death of sin.

---

[3] "Cadite super nos, et abscondite nos a facie sedentis super thronum, et ab ira Agni." — Apoc. vi. 16.

[4] "Quis ergo nos separabit a charitate Christi?" — Rom. viii. 35.

XX

Deus meus! Deus meus! Ut quid dereliquisti me?

"My God, my God, why hast Thou forsaken me?"
Matt. xxvii. 46.

O God! who shall not compassionate the Son of God, who for love of men is dying of grief on a cross? He is tormented externally in his body by the innumerable wounds, and internally he is so afflicted and sad that he seeks solace for his great sorrow from the Eternal Father; but his Father, in order to satisfy his divine justice, abandons him, and leaves him to die desolate and deprived of every consolation.

O desolate death of my dear Redeemer, Thou art my hope. O my abandoned Jesus, Thy merits make me hope that I shall not remain abandoned and separated from Thee forever in hell. I do not care to live in consolation on this earth; I embrace all the pains and desolations that Thou mayest send me. He is not worthy of consolation who by offending Thee has merited for himself eternal torments. It is enough for me to love Thee and to live in Thy grace. This alone do I beg of Thee, let me nevermore see myself deprived of Thy love. Let me be abandoned by all; do not Thou abandon me in this extremity. I love Thee, my Jesus, who didst die abandoned for me. I love Thee, my only good, my only hope, my only love.

XXI

Crucifixerunt eum, et cum eo alias duos hinc et hinc, medium autem Jesum.

"They crucified Him, and with Him two others, one on each side, and Jesus in the midst."
John xix. 18.

The incarnate Word was called by the sacred spouse, *All lovely; such is my beloved.*[1] At whatever period of his life Jesus Christ presents himself to us, he appears altogether desirable and most worthy of love, whether we see him as an infant in the stable, as a boy in the shop of St. Joseph, as a solitary meditating in the desert, or bathed in sweat as he walked about preaching throughout Judea. But in no other form does he appear more loving than when he is nailed to the cross on which the immense love he bears us forced him to die. St. Francis de Sales has said, the Mount of Calvary is the hill of lovers. All love which does not take its rise from the Passion of the Saviour is weak. How miserable is the death where there is no love of the Redeemer! Let us stop, then, and consider that this man, nailed to the tree of shame, is our true God, and that he is here suffering and dying for nothing but for the love of us.

---

[1] "Totus desiderabilis, talis est Dilectus meus." — *Cant.* v. 16.

Ah, my Jesus, if all men would stand still and contemplate Thee on the cross, believing with a lively faith, that Thou art their God, and that Thou hast died for their salvation, how could they live far from Thee and without Thy love? And how could I, knowing all this, have displeased Thee so often? If others have offended Thee, they have at least sinned in darkness; but I have sinned in the light. But these pierced hands, this wounded side, this blood, these wounds which I see in Thee, make me hope for pardon and Thy grace. I am grieved, my Love, for having ever so despised Thee. But now I love Thee with all my heart; and my greatest grief is the remembrance of my having despised Thee. This grief, however, which I feel, is a sign that Thou hast pardoned me. O burning heart of my Jesus, inflame my poor heart with Thy love. O my Jesus, dead, consumed with sorrow for me, make me die consumed with sorrow for having offended Thee, and with the love Thou dost merit, I sacrifice myself entirely to Thee, who hast sacrificed Thyself entirely for me. O sorrowful Mother Mary, make me faithful in loving Jesus!

XXII

Et inclinato capite, tradidit spiritum.

"And bowing His head, He gave up the ghost."
John xix. 30.

Behold, my Redeemer, to what Thy love for men has brought Thee – even to die of sorrow on a cross, drowned in a sea of grief and ignominy; as David had predicted of Thee. *I am come into the depth of the sea, and a tempest hath overwhelmed me.*[1] St. Francis de Sales writes thus: "Let us contemplate this divine Saviour stretched on the cross, as upon the altar of his glory, on which he is dying of love for us. Ah, why, then, do we not in spirit throw ourselves upon him to die upon the cross with him who has chosen to die there for the love of us? I will hold him, we ought to say; I will never let him go. I will die with him, and will burn in the flames of his love; one and the same fire shall devour this divine Creator and his miserable creature. My Jesus is all mine, and I am all his. I will live and die on his bosom. Neither life nor death shall ever separate me from my Jesus."[2]

Yes, my dear Redeemer, I hold fast to Thy cross; I kiss Thy pierced feet, touched with compassion and confounded at seeing the affection with which Thou hast died for me. Ah, accept me, and bind me to Thy feet, that I may no more

---

[1] "Veni in altitudinem maris, et tempestas demersit me." — Ps . lxviii. 3.
[2] *Love of God*, book vii., ch. 8.

depart from Thee, and may from this day forward converse with Thee alone, consult with Thee on all my thoughts; in a word, may I henceforth direct all my affections so as to seek nothing but to love Thee and please Thee, always longing to leave this valley of dangers to come and love Thee face to face with all my strength in Thy kingdom, which is a kingdom of eternal love. In the mean time let me always live, grieving for the offences I have committed against Thee, and always burning with love for Thee, who for love of me hast given Thy life. I love Thee, my Jesus, who hast died for me; I love Thee, O infinite lover; I love Thee, O infinite love; I love Thee, infinite goodness. O Mary, Mother of beautiful love, pray to my Jesus for me.

XXIII

Oblatus est, quia ipse voluit.

"He was offered because it was His own will."
Isa. liii. 7.

The incarnate Word, at the moment of his conception, saw before him all the souls that he was to redeem. Then thou also, my soul, wast presented with the guilt of all thy sins upon thee, and for thee did Jesus Christ accept all the pains that he suffered in life and death; and in doing so he obtained for thee thy pardon, and all the graces that thou hast received from God – the lights, the calls of his love, the helps to overcome temptations, the spiritual consolations, the tears, the compassionate feelings thou hast experienced when thinking of the love he had for thee, and the sentiments of sorrow in remembering how thou hast offended him.

Thou didst, then, my Jesus, from the very beginning of Thy life, take upon Thee all my sins, and didst offer Thyself to satisfy for them by Thy sufferings. By Thy death Thou hast delivered me from eternal death: *But Thou hast delivered my soul, that it should not perish; Thou hast cast all my sins behind Thy back.*[1] Thou, my love, instead of punishing me for the insults which I have added to those that Thou hadst already received, hast gone on adding to Thy favors and mercies

---

[1] "Tu autem eruisti animam meam, ut non periret; projecisti post tergum tuum omnia peccata mea." — Isa. xxxviii. 17.

towards me, in order to win my heart one day to Thyself. My Jesus, this day is come; I love Thee with all my soul. Who should love Thee if I do not? This is the first sin, my Jesus, that Thou hast to forgive me, that I have been so many years in the world without loving Thee. But for the future I will do all I can to please Thee.

I feel by Thy grace a great desire to live to Thee alone, and to detach myself from all created things, I have also a great compunction for the displeasure that I have caused Thee. This desire and this sorrow, I see, my Jesus, are all Thy gift. Continue, then, my love, to keep me faithful in Thy love; for Thou knowest my weakness. Make me all Thine, as Thou hast made Thyself all mine. I love Thee, my only good; I love Thee, my only love; I love Thee, my treasure, my all; My Jesus, I love Thee, I love Thee, I love Thee. Help me, O Mother of God.

XXIV

Deus Filium suum mittens in similitudinem carnis peccati, et de peccato damnavit peccatum in carne. Christus nos redentit de maledicto legis factus pro nobis maledictum, quia scriptum est: Maledictus omnis qui pendet in ligno.

"God sending his own Son in the likeness of sinful flesh, even of sin, hath condemned sin in the flesh."
Rom. viii. 3.
"Christ hath redeemed us from the curse of the law, being made a curse for us, for it is written: Cursed is every one that hangeth on a tree."
Gal. iii. 13.

Hence we see that Jesus Christ willed to appear in the world as a guilty and an accused man, hanging on the cross to deliver us from eternal malediction.

O eternal Father, for the love of this Son so dear to Thee, have pity on me! And Thou, Jesus, my Redeemer, who by Thy death hast liberated me from the slavery of sin in which I was born, and of the sins that I have committed since my baptism, ah, change the miserable chains which once bound me a slave to Satan into chains of gold, which may bind me to Thee with a holy love. Arise and show forth in me the efficacy of Thy merits, by changing me, a sinner, into a saint. I have deserved to be burning in hell for many years past: but I hope by Thy infinite mercy, for the glory of Thy death, to burn with Thy love, and to be all Thine. I wish that my heart should love none but Thee. *Thy kingdom come.* Reign, my Jesus, reign over my whole soul. May it obey Thee alone, seek Thee alone, desire Thee alone. Away from my heart, ye earthly affections! and come, O ye flames of divine love; come and remain alone to possess and consume me for that God of love who didst die consumed for me. I love Thee, my Jesus; I love Thee, O infinite Sweetness and my true lover, I have no one who has loved me more than Thou; and therefore I give and consecrate myself to Thee, my treasure and my all.

XXV

Dilexit nos, et lavit nos a peccatis nostris in sanguine suo.

"He hath loved us, and washed us from our sins in His own blood."
Apoc. i. 5.

So, then, my Jesus, in order to save my soul, Thou hast prepared a bath of Thine own blood wherein to cleanse it from the filth of its sins. If, then, our souls have been bought by Thy blood, *For you are bought with a great price,*[1] it is a sign that Thou lovest them much; and as Thou dost love them, let us pray thus to Thee: *We therefore pray Thee to help Thy servants, whom Thou hast redeemed with Thy precious blood.*[2] It is true that by my sins I have separated myself from Thee, and have knowingly lost Thee. But remember, my Jesus, that Thou hast bought me with Thy blood. Ah, may this blood not have been given in vain for me, which was shed with so much grief and so much love.

By my sins I have driven Thee, my God, from my soul, and have merited Thy hatred; but Thou hast said that Thou wouldst forget the crimes of a repentant sinner. *But if he do penance…I will not remember all his iniquities.*[3] Thou hast

---

[1] "Empti enim estis pretio magno." — I Cor. vi. 20.
[2] "Te ergo quaesumus, tuis famulis subveni, quos pretioso sanguine redemisti."
[3] "Si impius egerit poenitentiam…,omnium iniquitatum ejus…non recordabor." — Ezek. xviii. 21.

further said, *I love them that love me.*[4] I pray Thee, therefore, my Jesus, to forget all the injuries that I have offered Thee, and love me; whilst I also will now love Thee more than myself, and repent above all things for having offended Thee. Ah, my beloved Lord, for the sake of that blood which Thou hast shed for the love of me, hate me no longer, but love me. It is not enough for me that Thou shouldst only forgive me the chastisement I deserve, I desire to love Thee and to be loved by Thee. O God, who art all love, all goodness, unite me and bind me to Thyself, and permit not that I should ever be separated from Thee any more, and that thus I should deserve Thy hatred. No, my Jesus, my love, let it not be, I will be all Thine, and I desire that Thou shouldst be all mine.

---

[4] "Ego diligentes me diligo." — Prov. viii. 17.

XXVI

Humiliavit semetipsum, factus obediens usque ad mortem, mortem autem crucis.

"He humbled Himself, becoming obedient unto death; even the death of the cross."
Phil. ii. 8.

What great thing is that the martyrs have done in giving their lives for God, while this God has humbled himself to the death of the cross for their love? To render a just return for the death of a God, it would not be sufficient to sacrifice the lives of all men; the death of another God for his love would alone compensate for it. O my Jesus! allow me, a poor sinner, to say to Thee, with Thy true lover St. Francis of Assisi, "May I die, O Lord, for the love of Thy love, as Thou didst deign to die for the love of my love."[1]

Is it true, my Redeemer, that hitherto, for the love of my own pleasures, unhappy that I am!, I have renounced Thy love? Would that I had died before, and had never offended Thee! I thank Thee that Thou givest me time to love Thee in this life, that I may afterwards love Thee throughout all eternity. Ah, remind me continually, my Jesus, of the ignominious death that Thou hast suffered for me, that I may never forget to love Thee in consideration of the love that

---

[1] "Moriar, Domine, amore amoris tui, qui amore amoris mei dignatus es mori."

Thou hast borne me. I love Thee, infinite goodness; I love Thee, my supreme good; to Thee I give myself entirely, and by that love which caused Thee to die for me, do Thou accept my love, and let me die, destroy me, rather than ever permit me to leave off loving Thee. I will say to Thee, with St. Francis de Sales, "O eternal Love, my soul seeks Thee, and chooses Thee for all eternity. Come, O Holy Spirit, inflame our hearts with Thy love. Either to love or to die. To die to all other affections, to live only to the love of Jesus."[2]

---

[2] *Love of God*, book xii. ch. 13.

XXVII

Charitas enim Christi urget nos.

"The charity of Christ presseth us."
2 Cor. v. 14.

How tender and full of unction are the words with which St. Francis de Sales comments on this passage in his book of the divine love! "Hear Theotimus," he says; "nothing forces and presses the soul of man so much as love. If a man knows that he is loved by any one, he feels himself forced to love him; but if a peasant is loved by a lord, he is still more strongly forced; and if by a monarch, how much more so! Know, then, that Jesus, the true God, has loved us so far as to suffer death, even the death of the cross for us. Is not this to have our hearts put under a press, and to feel them squeezed and crushed so as to force out our love with a violence which is all the stronger for being so loving."

Ah, my Jesus, since Thou dost desire to be loved by me, remind me always of the love that Thou hast borne me, and of the pains Thou hast suffered to show me this love. May the remembrance of them be ever present in my mind and in the minds of all men, for it is impossible to believe what Thou hast suffered to oblige us to love, and yet not love Thee. Till now the cause of my negligent and wicked life has been, that I have not thought of the affection which Thou, my Jesus, hast had for me. All this time, however, I knew the great displeasure my sins gave Thee, and nevertheless I went on multiplying them. Every time I remember this I should wish to die of grief for it, and I should not now have courage to ask Thy pardon, if I did not know that Thou didst die to obtain forgiveness for me.

Thou hast borne with me in order that at the sight of the wrong I have done Thee, and of the death that Thou hast suffered for me, my sorrow and love towards Thee should be increased. I repent, my dear Redeemer, with all my heart, for having offended Thee, and I love Thee with all my soul. After so many signs of Thy affection, and after the many mercies that Thou hast shown me, I promise Thee that I will love none but Thee. Thee will I love with all my strength; Thou art my Jesus, my love, my all. Thou art my love, because in Thee I have placed all my affections. Thou art my all, because I will have none other but Thee. Grant, then, that always, both in life and death and through all eternity, I may ever call Thee my God, my love, and my all.

XXVIII

Charitas enim Christi urget nos.

"The charity of Christ presseth us."
2 Cor. v. 14.

Let us consider anew the force of these words. The Apostle means to say that it is not so much the thought of all that Christ has suffered for us that should constrain us to love him, as the thought of the love that he has shown us in wishing to suffer so much for us. This love made our Saviour say, while he was yet alive, that he was dying with the desire that the day of his death should draw near to make us know the boundless love that he had for us. *I have a baptism wherewith I am to be baptized, and how am I straitened till it be accomplished!*[1] And the same love made him say the last night of his life. *With desire, I have desired to eat this pasch with you before I suffer.*[2]

So great, then, my Jesus, was the desire that Thou hadst to be loved by us, that all through Thy life Thou didst desire nothing but to suffer and to die for us, and so to put us under the necessity of loving Thee at least out of gratitude for so much love. Dost Thou so thirst for our love? How is it, then,

---
[1] "Baptismo habeo baptizari; et quomodo coarctor, usquedum perficiatur!" — Luke xii. 50.
[2] "Desiderio desideravi hoc pascha manducare vobiscum, antequam patiar." — Ibid. xxii. 15.

that we so little desire Thine. Alas, that I should have been up to this time so foolish! Not only have I not desired Thy love, but I have brought down upon myself Thy hatred by losing my respect for Thee.

My dear Redeemer, I know the evil I have done, I detest it above all my other sins, and am sorry from the bottom of my heart. Now I desire Thy love more than all the goods of the world. My best and only treasure, I love Thee above all things, I love Thee more than myself, I love Thee with all my soul, and I desire nothing but to love Thee and to be loved by Thee. Forget, my Jesus, the offences that I have committed against Thee; do Thou also love me, and love me exceedingly, that I may exceedingly love Thee. Thou art my love, Thou art my hope, Thou knowest how weak I am; help me, Jesus, my love; help me, Jesus, my hope. Succor me also with thy prayers, O Mary, great Mother of God.

XXIX

Majorem hac dilectionem nemo habet, ut animam suam ponat quis pro amicis suis.

"Greater love than this no man hath, that a man lay down his life for his friends."
John xv. 13.

What more, O my soul! could thy God do than to give his life in order to make thee love him? To give his life is the greatest mark of affection that a man can give to another man who is his friend. But what love must that have been which our Creator has shown to us, in choosing to die for us his creatures! This is what St. John was considering when he wrote: *In this we have known the charity of God, because He hath laid down His life for us.*[1] Indeed, if faith did not teach us that a God has willed to die to show us his love, who would ever have been able to believe it?

Ah, my Jesus, I believe that Thou hast died for me, and therefore I confess that I deserve a thousand hells for having repaid with insults and ingratitude the love that Thou hast borne me in giving Thy life for me. I thank Thy mercy, which has promised to forgive those that repent. Trusting, then, in this sweet promise, I hope for pardon from Thee, repenting, as I do, with all my heart for having so often despised Thy

---

[1] "In hoc cognovimus charitatem Dei, quoniam ille animam suam pro nobis posuit." — I John iii. 16.

love. But since Thy love has not abandoned me, overcome by Thy love I consecrate myself all to Thee. Thou, my Jesus, hast finished Thy life by dying in agony on a cross; and what recompense can I, a miserable creature, make Thee? I consecrate to Thee my life, accepting with love all the sufferings that will come to me from Thy hand, both in life and in death. Softened and confounded at the great mercy that Thou hast used towards me, I hold fast Thy cross; at Thy feet will I thus live and die. Ah, my Redeemer, by the love that Thou hast borne me in dying for me, do not permit me ever to separate myself from Thee again. Make me always live and die in Thy embrace. My Jesus, my Jesus, I repeat, make me always live and die united with Thee.

XXX

Et ego, si exaltatus fuero a terra, omnia traham ad me ipsum.

"I, if I be lifted up from the earth, will draw all things unto Myself."
John xii. 32.

Thou hast said, then, my Saviour, that when hanging on the cross Thou wouldst draw all our hearts unto Thyself; why is it that for so many years my heart has gone far away from Thee? Ah, it is not Thy fault. How many times hast Thou called me to Thy love and I have turned a deaf ear? How many times too hast Thou pardoned me, and affectionately warned me by remorse of conscience not to offend Thee again, and I have repeated my offence? Ah, my Jesus, send me not to hell, because there I shall be cursing forever these graces which Thou hast given me; so that these graces, the illuminations Thou hast given me, Thy calls, Thy patience in bearing with me, the blood that Thou didst shed to save me, would be the most cruel of all the torments of hell. But now I hear Thee call me again, and Thou dost say to me, with the greatest love, as if I had never offended Thee: *Love the Lord Thy God with all thy heart.*[1] Thou dost command me to love Thee, and to love Thee with all my heart.

---

[1] "Diliges Dominum Deum timm ex toto corde tuo." — Matt. xxii. 37.

But if Thou didst not command me, O Jesus! how could I live without loving Thee, after so many proofs of Thy love? Yes, I love Thee, my supreme good; I love Thee with all my heart. I love Thee because Thou dost command me to love Thee. I love Thee because Thou art worthy of infinite love. I love Thee, and desire nothing else but to love Thee, and nothing else do I fear except being separated from Thee, and living without Thy love. Ah, my crucified love, permit not that I ever leave off loving Thee. Ever call to my remembrance the death that Thou hast undergone for me. Remind me of the endearments that Thou hast used towards me, and may the remembrance of them incite me more and more to love Thee, and to spend myself for Thee, who hast spent Thyself as a victim of love on the cross for me.

XXXI

Qui etiam proprio Filio suo non pepercit, sed pro nobis omnibus tradidit illum quomodo non etiam cum illo omnia nobis donavit?

"He that spared not His only Son, but delivered Him up for us all, how hath He not also . . . given us all things?"
Rom. viii. 32.

What flames of love ought not these words enkindle in our hearts: *Delivered Him up for us all!*[1] Divine justice, offended by our sins, must be satisfied; what, therefore, does God do? To pardon us, he wills that his Son should be condemned to death, and should himself pay the penalty due from us: *He spared not His only Son.*[2] O God! if the eternal Father were capable of suffering, what grief would he not have experienced in condemning to death, for the sins of his servants, his well-beloved and innocent Son! Let us imagine that we see the eternal Father, with Jesus dead in his arms, and saying, *For the wickedness of My people have I struck Him.*[3] Rightly did St. Francis of Paula exclaim, in ecstasy of love, when meditating on the death of Jesus Christ, "O love! O love! O love!" On the other hand, with what confidence should not the following words inspire us: *How hath He not also, with*

---

[1] "Pro nobis omnibus tradidit illum." — Rom. viii. 32.
[2] "Proprio Filio non pepercit." — Rom. viii. 32.
[3] "Propter scelus populi mei percuss! eum." — Isa. liii. 8.

Him, given us all things?[4] And how, my God, should I fear that Thou shouldst not give me pardon, perseverance, Thy love, Thy Paradise, and all the graces that I can hope for, now that Thou hast given me that which is most dear to Thee, even Thine own Son? I know what I must do to obtain every good from Thee, – I must ask for it for the love of Jesus Christ; of this Jesus Christ himself assures me: *Amen, amen, I say to you, if you ask the Father anything in My name, He will give it you.*[5]

My supreme and eternal God, I have hitherto despised Thy majesty and goodness; now I love Thee above all things; and because I love Thee, I repent with all my heart of having offended Thee, and would rather accept any chastisement than evermore offend Thee. Pardon me, and grant me those graces which I now ask of Thee, confiding in the promise of Jesus Christ. In the name of Jesus Christ I beseech Thee to give me holy perseverance to death, give me a pure and perfect love towards Thee, give me an entire conformity to Thy holy will, give me finally Paradise. I ask for all, and hope for all, from Thee through the merits of Jesus Christ. I deserve nothing; I am worthy of punishment, not of graces, but Thou dost deny nothing to those who pray to Thee for the love of Jesus Christ. Ah, my good God, I see that Thou dost wish me to be all Thine; I also wish to be Thine, and will not fear that my sins should prevent me from being all Thine, – Jesus Christ has already satisfied for them, – and Thou, besides, art ready, for the love of Jesus Christ, to give me all that I desire. This is my desire and my request; my God, hear me! I wish to love Thee, to love Thee exceedingly; and to be altogether Thine. Most holy Mary, help me.

---

[4] "Quomodo non etiam cum illo omnia nobis donavit?" — Rom. viii. 32.
[5] "Amen, amen dico vobis: si quid petieritis Patrem in nomine meo, dabit vobis." — John xvi. 23.

XXXII

Nos autem praedicamus Christum crucifixum, Judaeis quidem scandalum, Gentibus autem stultitiam.

"But we preach Christ crucified, unto the Jews indeed a stumbling-block, and unto the Gentiles foolishness."
I Cor. i. 23.

St. Paul assures us that the Gentiles, hearing it preached that the Son of God had been crucified for the salvation of mankind, reckoned it folly: *But unto the Gentiles foolishness;*[1] as if they said, Who can believe such folly, that a God should have willed to die for the love of his creatures! "It seems a foolish thing," says St. Gregory, "that a God should wish to die for the salvation of man."[2] St. Mary Magdalen of Pazzi, also rapt in love, exclaims in an ecstasy, Do you not know, my sisters, that my Jesus is nothing but love? Rather he is mad with love. I say that Thou art mad with love, my Jesus, and I will always say so.

My beloved Redeemer, oh that I could possess the hearts of all men, and with them love Thee as Thou deservest to be loved! O God of love, why, after Thou hast shed all Thy blood in this world and given Thy life for the love of mankind, – why, I say, are there so few men who burn with Thy love?

---

[1] "Gentibus autem stultitiam." — i Cor. i. 23.
[2] "Stultum visum est ut pro hominibus Auctor vitae moreretur.' — In Evang. hom. 6.

For this end didst Thou come, namely, to kindle in our hearts the fire of Thy love, and Thou desirest nothing but to see it enkindled. *I am come to cast fire on the earth, and what will I but that it be kindled?*[3] I pray, then, with the Holy Church, in my name and in the name of every one living, kindle in them the fire of Thy love; enkindle them, enkindle them, enkindle them!

My God, Thou art all goodness, all love, all infinite sweetness, boundless in love; make Thyself known to all, make Thyself loved. I am not ashamed of praying thus to Thee, although up to this time I have been more guilty than others in despising Thy love, – because now, enlightened by Thy grace, and wounded by the many arrows of love Thou hast shot forth from Thy burning and loving heart into my soul, I am determined no longer to be ungrateful to Thee as I have hitherto been; but I will love Thee with all my strength, I desire to burn with Thy love, and this Thou hast to grant me. I look not for sensible consolations in loving Thee; I do not deserve them, neither do I ask for them; it is enough for me to love Thee. I love Thee, my sovereign good; I love Thee, my God and my all.

---

[3] "Ignem veni mittere in terram: et quid volo, nisi ut accendatur?" — Luke xii. 49.

XXXIII

Posuit Dominus in eo iniquitatem omnium nostrum…, et voluit conterere eum.

"The Lord hath laid on Him the iniquity of us all…And the Lord hath pleased to bruise Him."
Isa. liii. 6, 10.

Behold the extent of divine love towards man! The eternal Father loads the shoulders of his Son with our sins; *And He was pleased to bruise Him.*[1] He willed that his own Son should suffer with the utmost rigor all the punishment due to us, making him die on an ignominious cross overwhelmed with torments. The apostle is just, then, when speaking of this love, to call it too much love to ordain that we should receive life through the death of his beloved Son. *For His exceeding charity wherewith He loved us, even when we were dead in sins, hath quickened us together in Christ.*[2]

Thou hast, then, my God, loved me too much, and I have been too ungrateful in offending Thee and turning my back upon Thee. Ah, eternal Father, look upon Thine only-begotten, mangled and dead upon that cross for me, and for the love of him pardon me and draw my heart wholly to Thyself to love Thee. *A contrite and humble heart, O God, thou*

---

[1] "Et voluit conterere eum."
[2] "Propter nimiam charitatem suam qua dilexit nos, et cum essemus mortui peccatis, convivificavit nos in Christo." — Eph. ii. 5.

wilt not despise.[3] For the love of Jesus Christ who died for our sins, Thou canst not despise a soul that humbles itself and repents. I know myself to be deserving of a thousand hells, but I repent with my whole heart for having offended Thee, the supreme Good. Reject me not, but have pity on me.

But I am not content with a simple pardon; I desire that Thou shouldst give me a great love towards Thee, that I may compensate for all the offences that I have committed against Thee. I love Thee, infinite Goodness, I love Thee, O God of love. It is but little if I should die and annihilate myself for Thy sake. I desire to know how to love Thee as Thou deservest. But Thou knowest I can do nothing; do Thou make me grateful for the immense love that Thou hast had for me. I beg this of Thee for the love of Jesus, Thy Son. Grant that I may overcome everything in this life to please Thee, and that in death I may expire entirely united to Thy will, and so come to love Thee face to face with a perfect and eternal love in Paradise.

---

[3] "Cor contritum et humiliatum, Deus, non despicies." – Ps. l. 19.

XXXIV

Ego sum Pastor bonus. Bonus Pastor animam suam dat pro ovibus suis.

"I am the Good Shepherd. The good shepherd giveth his life for his sheep."
John x. ii.

My Jesus, what dost Thou say? What shepherd would ever give his life for his sheep? Thou alone, because Thou art a God of infinite love, canst say, *And I lay down My life for My sheep.*[1] Thou alone hast been able to show to the world this excess of love, that being our God and our supreme Lord, Thou hast yet willed to die for us. It was of this excess of love that Moses and Elias spoke on Mount Tabor: *They spoke of his decease that he should accomplish in Jerusalem.*[2] Hence St. John exhorts us to love a God who was the first to love us: *Let us therefore love God because God first hath loved us.*[3] As if he said, If we will not love this God for his infinite goodness, let us love him at least for the love that he has borne us in suffering willingly the pains that were due to us.

Remember, then, my Jesus, that I am one of those sheep for whom Thou hast given Thy life. Ah, cast on me one of those looks of pity with which Thou didst regard me once

---

[1] "Et animam meam pono pro ovibus meis." — John x. 15.
[2] "Dicebant excessum ejus, quem completurus erat in Jerusalem." — Luke ix. 31.
[3] "Nos ergo diligamus eum, quoniam Deus prior dilexit nos." – I John iv. 19.

when Thou wast dying on the cross for me; look on me, change me, and save me. Thou hast called Thyself the loving Shepherd who, finding the lost sheep, takes it with joy and carries it on his shoulders, and then calls his friends to rejoice with him: *Rejoice with me, for I have found the sheep that was lost.*[4] Behold, I am the lost sheep; seek me and find me: *I have gone astray like a sheep that is lost; seek Thy servant.*[5] If through my fault Thou hast not yet found me, take me now and unite me and bind me to Thee, that Thou mayest not lose me again. The bond must be that of Thy love; if Thou dost not bind me with this sweet chain Thou wilt again lose me. Ah, it is not Thou who hast been wanting in binding me by holy love; but I, an ungrateful wretch, who have continually fled from Thee.

But now I pray Thee, by that infinite mercy which caused Thee to come down to the earth to find me. Ah, bind me; but bind me with a double chain of love, that Thou mayest not lose me again, and that I may no more lose Thee. I renounce all the goods and pleasures of the world, and offer myself to suffer every pain, every death, provided that I live and die always united to Thee. I love Thee, my sweet Jesus; I love Thee, my good Shepherd, who hast died for Thy lost sheep; but know that this sheep now loves Thee more than himself, and desires nothing but to love Thee and to be consumed by Thy love. Have pity on him, then, and permit him never again to be separated from Thee.

---

[4] "Congratulamini mihi, quia inveni ovem meam quae perierat."- Luke xv. 6.
[5] "Erravi sicut ovis quae periit; quaere servum tuum." — Ps. cxviii. 176.

XXXV

Ego pono animam meam...Nemo tollit eam a me, sed ego pono eam a meipso.

"I lay down My life...No one taketh it away from Me; but I lay it down of Myself."
John x. 17, 18.

Behold, then, the Word Incarnate, urged alone by the love that he preserves towards us, accepts the death of the cross to give to man the life that he had lost. Behold, says St. Thomas, a God does for man more than he could have done if man had been (so to speak) his God, and as if God could never have been happy without man. "As if," these are the words of the saint, "man had been God's god, as if God could not be happy without him."[1] We sinned, and by sinning merited eternal punishment; and what does Jesus do? He takes upon himself the obligation of satisfaction, and he pays for us by his sufferings and his death: *Surely he hath borne our infirmities and carried our sorrows.*[2]

Ah, my Jesus, since I have been the cause of all the bitterness and anguish that Thou didst suffer while living on this earth, I pray Thee make me share the grief that Thou

---

[1] "Quasi homo Dei Deus esset, quasi sine ipso beatus esse non posset." — *Opusc.* 63, c. 7.
[2] "Vere languores nostros ipse tulit, et dolores nostros ipse portavit." — Isa. liii. 4.

didst feel for my sins, and give me confidence in Thy Passion. What would have become of me, my Lord, if Thou hadst not deigned to satisfy for me? O infinite Majesty, I repent with my whole heart for having outraged Thee; but I hope for pity from Thee, who art infinite Goodness. Arise, O Saviour of the world, and apply to my soul the fruit of Thy death, and from an ungrateful rebel make me become such a true son as to love Thee alone, and to fear nothing but to displease Thee.

May that same love which made Thee die on the cross for me destroy in me all earthly affections. My Jesus, take my whole body to Thyself in such a way that it may only serve to obey Thee; take my heart, that it may desire nothing but Thy pleasure; take my whole will, that it may wish for nothing but what is according to Thy will. I embrace Thee and press Thee to my heart, my Redeemer. Ah, do not disdain to unite Thyself to me. I love Thee, O God of love. I love Thee, my only good. How could I have the heart to leave Thee again, now that Thou hast taught me how much Thou hast loved me, and how many mercies Thou hast shown me, changing the punishments that were due to me into graces and caresses? O holy Virgin, obtain for me the grace of being grateful to thy Son.

XXXVI

Delens quod adversus nos erat chirographum decreti, quod erat contrarium nobis, et ipsum tulit de medio, affigens illud cruci.

"Blotting out the handwriting of the decree that was against us, which was contrary to us. And he hath taken the same out of the way, fastening it to the cross."
Coloss. ii. 14.

The sentence was already recorded against us that was to condemn us to eternal death, as rebels of the offended Majesty of God. And what has Jesus Christ done? With his blood he has cancelled the writing of the condemnation, and, to deliver us from all fear, he has fastened it to his own cross, on which he died to satisfy for us to the divine justice. My soul, behold the obligation that thou art under to thy Redeemer; and hear how the Holy Spirit now reminds thee: *Forget not the kindness of thy surety.*[1] Forget not the kindness of thy surety, who, taking upon himself thy debts, has paid them for thee; and behold, the pledge of the payment has been already fixed to the cross. When, therefore thou dost remember thy sins, look upon the cross, and have confidence; look on that sacred wood stained with the blood of the Lamb of God sacrificed for thy love, and hope in and love a God who has loved thee so much.

---

[1] "Gratiam fidejussoris ne obliviscaris; dedit enim pro te animam suam." — Ecclus. xxix. 20.

Yes, my Jesus, I hope everything from Thy infinite goodness. It is property of Thy divine nature to render good for evil to those who repent of their sins, are sorry for having committed them, and who love Thee. Yes, I am sorry above all things, my beloved Redeemer, for having so much despised Thy goodness, and, wounded by Thy love, I love Thee, and I ardently desire to please Thee in everything that is Thy will. Alas! when I was in sin, I was the servant of the devil, and he was my master. Now that I hope to remain in Thy grace, Thou alone, my Jesus, art the only Lord of my heart, and my only Love. Take possession of me, then; keep me always, possess me entirely; for Thine only do I desire to be. No, nevermore will I forget the pains that Thou hast suffered for me; so shall I be more and more inflamed, and increase in Thy love. I love Thee, my most dear Redeemer; I love Thee, O Word Incarnate; my treasure, my all, I love Thee, I love Thee.

XXXVII

Si quis peccaverit, advocatum habemus apud Patrem Jesum Christum justum, et ipse est propitiatio pro peccatis nostris.

"But if any man sin, we have an Advocate with the Father, Jesus Christ the Just, and he is the propitiation for our sins."
I John II. I.

Oh, what great confidence do these words give to penitent sinners! Jesus Christ is in heaven, advocating their cause, and he is certain to obtain pardon for them. The devil, when a sinner has escaped from his chains, tempts him to be diffident of obtaining pardon. But St. Paul encourages him, saying, *Who is He that shall condemn? Jesus Christ that died,…who also maketh intercession for us.*[1] The Apostle means to say, If we detest the sins that we have committed, why do we fear? Who is he who will condemn us? It is Jesus Christ, the same who died, that we might *not* be condemned, and who is now in heaven, where he is advocating our cause. He goes on to say, *Who then shall separate us from the love of Christ?*[2] As if he would say, But after we have been pardoned with so much love by Jesus Christ, and have been received into his grace, who could have the heart to turn his back upon him, and separate himself from his love?

---

[1] "Quis est qui condemnet? Christus Jesus, qui mortuus est,…qui etiam interpellat pro nobis." — Rom. viii. 34.
[2] "Quis ergo nos separabit a charitate Christi?" — Rom. viii. 35.

No, my Jesus, I no longer rely upon myself so as to live separated from Thee and deprived of Thy love. I weep over the unhappy days when I lived without Thy grace. Now I hope that Thou hast pardoned me. I love Thee, and Thou lovest me. But Thou dost love with a boundless love, and I love Thee so little; give me more love. Infinite Goodness, I repent above all things for having hitherto so ill-treated Thee; now I love Thee above all things, I love Thee more than myself; and I take more delight, my God, in knowing that Thou art infinitely blessed than in my own happiness, because I love Thee better – being, as Thou art, worthy of infinite love – than myself, who deserve nothing but hell. My Jesus, I wish for nothing from Thee, but Thyself.

XXXVIII

Venite ad me omnes, qui laboratis et onerati estis, et ego reficiam vos.

"Come to Me, all you that labor, and are burdened, and I will refresh you."
Matt. xi. 28.

Let us listen to Jesus Christ, who from the cross to which he is nailed, and from the altar where he dwells under the sacramental species, calls us poor afflicted sinners to console us and enrich us with his graces. Oh, what two great mysteries of hope and love to us are the Passion of Jesus Christ and the Sacrament of the Eucharist! – mysteries which, if faith did not make us certain of them, would be incredible. That God should deign to shed even the very last drop of his blood! (for this is the signification of *effundetur*). *This is My Blood,…which shall be shed for many.*[1] And why? To atone for our sins. But then to will to give his own body as food for our souls, – that body which had already been sacrificed on the cross for our salvation! These sublime mysteries must surely soften the hardest hearts, and raise up the most desperate sinners. Finally, the Apostle says that in Jesus Christ we are enriched with every good, so that no grace is wanting to us: *In all things you are made rich in*

---

[1] "Hic est sanguis meus, qui pro multis effundetur." — Matt. xxvi. 28.

*Him...So that nothing is wanting to you in any grace.*² It is enough that we invoke this God for him to have mercy on us; and he will abound in grace to all who pray to him, as the same Apostle assures us: *Rich unto all who call upon Him.*³

If, then, my Saviour, I have reason to despair of pardon for the offences and treacheries that I have been guilty of towards Thee, I have still greater reason to trust in Thy goodness. My Father, I have forsaken Thee, like an ungrateful son; but I now return to Thy feet, full of sorrow and covered with confusion for the many mercies that Thou hast shown me; and I say with shame, *Father, I am not worthy to be called Thy son.*⁴ Thou hast said that there is rejoicing in heaven when a sinner is converted: *There shall be joy in heaven upon one sinner that doth penance.*⁵ Behold, I leave all and turn to Thee, my crucified Father; I repent with my whole heart for having treated Thee with such contempt as to turn my back upon Thee. Receive me again to Thy grace, and inflame with Thy holy love, so that I may never leave Thee again.

Thou hast said, *I am come that they may have life, and may have it more abundantly.*⁶ Wherefore I hope to receive from Thee, not only Thy grace as I enjoyed it before I offended Thee, but a grace more abundant, which shall make me become all on fire with Thy love. Oh that I could love Thee, my God, as Thou dost deserve to be loved! I love Thee above all things. I love Thee more than myself. I love Thee with all my heart; and I aspire after heaven, where I shall love Thee for all eternity. *What is there to me in heaven, and besides Thee what have I desired on earth? O God, God of my heart and my portion forever.*⁷ Ah, God of my heart, take and keep possession of all my heart, and drive from it every affection

---

² "In omnibus divites facti estis in illo...ita ut nihil vobis desit in ulla gratia." — I Cor. i. 5.
³ "Dives in omnes qui invocant illum." — Rom. x. 12.
⁴ "Pater, non sum dignus vocari filius tuus." — Luke xv. 21.
⁵ "Gaudium erit in coelo super uno peccatore poenitentiam agente." — Luke xv. 7.
⁶ "Veni ut vitam habeant, et abundantius habeant. " — John x. 10.
⁷ "Quid enim mihi est in coelo? et a te quid volui super terram? ...Deus cordis mei, et pars mea, Deus, in aeternum." — Ps. lxxii.

that does not belong to Thee. Thou art my only treasure, my only love. I wish for Thee alone, and nothing more. O Mary, my hope, by thy prayers draw me all to God.

From the Publisher:

the following is a two-part Summary

of Daily Counsel

&

of Essential Wisdom

from
A Christian's Rule of Life

Summary

A Curated Selection of the Daily Counsel of Saint Alphonsus Liguori[1]

In the Morning

I. Upon Rising
   a. Offer the prayers on page 21-23
II. Daily Meditation
   a. Thirty Minutes
   b. The morning is the best time.
   c. Meditate on the Four Last Things: Death, Judgment, Heaven, and Hell. If this is done, as Sacred Scripture says, a man will sin no more.
   d. A book is recommended to be used for meditation. *Darts of Fire* is highly recommended by St. Alphonsus Liguori.[2]
   e. A book may be used in the beginning of the meditation. The Christian should use a book which touches his soul but, in this, imitate the bees who settle on a flower as long they find any honey in it, and then pass on to another.
   f. Within the meditation, among other things remember to repeat acts of love and contrition which merit for the soul the grace of God and eternal life.

---

[1] This section is a collection of the wisdom of this great Saint and the majority of the content here is a summary and paraphrasing of the Saint's own words. Only the content which is presented within quotation marks is the original wording of St. Alphonsus Liguori.
[2] See the *Introduction* to *Darts of Fire*.

      g. Even in a state of aridity, a simple and contrite prayer will cause the prayer to succeed exceedingly well.
      h. Prayer should end with the making of a resolution, such as the avoidance of a specific sin.
      i. Fifteen-Thirty Minutes
          i. Read the life of a Saint

Throughout the Day

III. Ask Our Lord for His graces and His divine assistance.
      a. Pray often and everywhere with humility, confidence, and perseverance.
      b. Confidently ask Jesus Christ, and His Mother, to help you obtain the graces necessary for salvation, in particular the grace to persevere until death.
      c. The two principal graces which we must ask of God are the love of God and holy perseverance.
          i. See page 43 for two ideal prayers
      d. Employ prayers like "Incline unto my aid, O God! O Lord, make Haste to help me!" or "My Jesus, mercy," asking for the love of God and holy perseverance. We should also ask the same graces from Mary.
      e. Offer short prayers at specific times throughout the day, such as when beginning work, when eating, at the beginning of each hour of the day, when aware of a sin, among others.
          i. See page 22 for these prayers

At Bedtime

IV. Make an examination of conscience by thanking God for all the favors you have received, then review your actions and words of the day, repenting of all faults.

V. Make the Christian acts of Faith, Hope, and Charity as presented on page 39 – 41.

VI. Afterward, pray the Rosary and the Litany of the Blessed Virgin Mary.

Each Day of the Week
VII. We should always turn to the Blessed Virgin Mary, the dispenser of all graces, asking for her help in obtaining these, for whatever she seeks, she finds.
    a. Beginning on page 45, St. Alphonsus presents seven prayers to Our Lady, one for each day of the week.
VIII. Seek to hear Mass every day.[3]
IX. A visit to Our Lord in the Most Blessed Sacrament and to Our Lady should be made every day.
    a. Beginning on page 37, St. Alphonsus presents two great prayers when visiting Our Lord and His Holy Mother in the Church.

Weekly
X. Frequent Confession
    a. Before Confession, beg for the light from God to enable you to know your sins, obtain the grace for true sorrow, and a firm purpose of amendment.
    b. Recommend yourself to Our Lady of Sorrows and offer the prayer on page 28 before making your Confession.
        i. See page 29 for a prayer to be said after Confession.
XI. Frequent Holy Communion
    a. We must focus on the ends for which the Mass was instituted which are 1) to honor God, 2) to thank Him for His benefits, 3) to satisfy for our sins, and 4) to obtain graces.
    b. Use the prayer on page 36 to help focus on this during Mass.

---

[3] Often, this is not possible. In this case, ask Our Lord for the grace to be united to the Holy Mass that day and to one day more easily be able to attend.

c. See page 30-34 for prayers to be said before and after Holy Communion.

Summary

A Curated Selection of the Wisdom of Saint Alphonsus Liguori[1]

God has given us all the means we need to conquer the assaults of our enemies and our disordered passions. Though all men desire to be saved, only those who employ these means will obtain their salvation.

~
Humility
~

It is best to avoid speaking about ourselves, whether the good that we do or the faults and sins that we commit.

Anger at a fall into sin is not humble and the devil can use this against us to prevent us from continuing to pursue the good. We must simply rise again with an act of love and contrition and resolve not to fall into that sin again.

When we see another fall into sin, we must simply pity them, pray for them, and ask God to continue to protect us with His grace.

---

[1] This section is a collection of the wisdom of this great Saint and the majority of the content here is a summary and paraphrasing of the Saint's own words. Only the content which is presented within quotation marks is the original wording of St. Alphonsus Liguori.

It is essential that we come to hold ourselves as the worst of all sinners, even if, in truth, our sins are not as grievous as those of others. For us, having received so many favors and graces from God, the sins which we commit are even more displeasing to God than those of others.

Humility should reach the will as well, such that we are pleased when we are despised by others.

The truly humble man does not grumble against being admonished for a fault, even for a fault that is not his. Instead, he receives it well and without anger, thanking the one who corrected him, even remaining silent and simply offering it all to God. In this we share in the ill-treatment which Our Lord received and imitate Him in His manner of responding.

~
Mortification
~

Mortification enables us to conquer our passions, in particular those vices which predominate. With a resolute will and the help of God, there is no vice which cannot be eradicated.

While it is principally necessary to mortify the will, the senses (the flesh) must also be mortified. When the flesh is not mortified, it is difficult to be obedient to God.

We must abstain from looking at anything that gives the occasion for temptation.

We must also mortify our tongue which, even when used to jest, can, by the inclusion of an impure word, or a word with a double meaning, do great harm and lead to the emergence of countless sins as its fruit.

The taste must also be mortified, for man tends to center his life around eating, endangering the health of both his body and his soul.

Be sure to fast and abstain from time to time, but in particular when obligated.[2]

~ Charity Toward Neighbor ~

If a man loves God, he will also love his neighbor.

Charity toward our neighbor begins interiorly by desiring our neighbor's good, rejoicing when he possesses it, and feeling sorry for misfortunes he may suffer.

Except if there should be good grounds, we must never judge nor suspect evil of our neighbor.

Exteriorly, we must speak well of our neighbor and, if a fault cannot be excused, we must at least excuse the intention behind it.

We must not relay to a person any evil that may have been said about him, always avoiding potentially sowing discord, an act which Scripture says is despised by God.

Our speech to our neighbor, even when speaking in jest, must be prudent lest we potentially hurt him by what we say. Our speech should be gentle at all times, meek in the face of abuse,

---

[2] Though, in modern times, the obligatory fasts are greatly reduced from the times in which St. Alphonsus lived. To fulfill his advice, it would be necessary to embrace more frequent fasting. - CDF

avoiding arguing and contradicting, stating our opinions and then being silent.

When we are angry it is best to wait until our passions have calmed before seeking to give a correction that may be necessary.

A most meritorious form of charity is almsgiving, understood by St. Alphonsus as any assistance which we are able to lend to our neighbor.

Charity to our neighbor includes our enemies as well. Seeking the good for our enemies is both a fulfillment of the command of Our Lord and a sign that the soul is loved by God.

Charity also includes love for the holy souls in Purgatory, those same neighbors who once lived among us but who are now helpless and suffering in prison.

~
Patience
~

"This earth is a place where we can gain merit; therefore it is not a place of rest, but of labors and sufferings; and it is for this end that God makes us live here, that by patience we may obtain the glory of paradise."

Patient endurance of sufferings, both internal and external, is a sign that the soul possesses a true love for Jesus Christ.

Sickness affords us a prime opportunity for the exercise of patience, and it is a moment in which the quality of our devotion is revealed. Just as we fulfill our obligations to God when we are well, such as when we go to Church, so we also fulfill His will when we patiently accept being confined to a sick bed.

The grief we experience at the death of a loved one should also be tempered by an acceptance of God's will. Grief that leads a person to cease their prayers and devotions and reduce their frequenting of the sacraments is not pleasing to the deceased nor to God.

Patience calls us to accept poverty we may face and say, "My God, Thou alone art sufficient for me."

Patient endurance in times of persecutions and spiritual desolations will conform us more perfectly to Jesus Christ and increase the reward awaiting us in Heaven. It is essential that we do not neglect prayer during this time.

In times of temptation, while we should beg Our Lord to deliver us from them, we should also patiently endure them, knowing that they are permitted for our spiritual good and perfection, and not for our damnation.

"And when the temptation continues, let us not cease to pray, saying: 'Jesus, help me! Mary, ever Virgin, assist me!' The mere invocation of these all-powerful names of Jesus and Mary will suffice to defeat the most violent assaults of hell. It is also of great use to make the sign of the cross on our forehead, or over our heart."

~
Conformity of the Will
~

When we conform ourselves to the will of God, accepting all that befalls us as willed by Him, all bitterness within our sufferings is removed. When we accept them in this way, they become moments of merit and riches for paradise.

Death, for example, when it is accepted in order that the will of God may be fulfilled, merits for us a reward similar to that of the martyrs, who also accepted death to please God.

"He who dies in union with the will of God makes a holy death; and the more closely he is united to it, the more holy death does he die. The Venerable Blosius declares that an act of perfect conformity to the will of God at the hour of death not only delivers us from hell, but also from purgatory."

"St. Teresa says: 'If you are willing to bear only those crosses for which you see a reason, perfection is not for you'."

"Generally speaking, this should be the continual tenor of our prayers, offering ourselves to God, that he may do with us as he pleases; saying to him in our prayers, our Communions, and in the visit: 'My God, make me do Thy will.' In doing the will of God we shall do everything."

We must unite ourselves to God's will regarding our natural defects, lack of talents, weak health, and the like. It is easy to see that many, with their natural talents, have been damned on their account. In the end, it should more than suffice that God has given us the good things that He has, and, even more, that He has called us into the Holy Faith.

When crosses of any form, and from any source, should come to us, we must accept them as coming from God as part of His work of perfecting our souls. These crosses can come through the sins of others against us. While God never wills or desires these sins, He does will the suffering that comes to us by means of these people. We must be willing to accept all adversities and persecutions.

If we resign ourselves to the will of God in times of dryness in prayer, yet continue with our devotions, we shall gain more in one day of this desolation than in a month of consolation. It is here that we are humbled before God, knowing that we do not deserve to experience His sweetness in prayer, but desiring still to be united to His love.

~
Purity of Intention
~

"Further, whenever we have done some good in order to please God, let us not torment ourselves in endeavoring to drive away vain-glory; if we are praised for it, it is enough to say: 'To God be the honor and glory.' And let us never omit doing any good action which may be edifying to our neighbor, through fear of vain-glory. Our Lord wishes us to do good even before others, that it may be profitable to them."

"Purity of intention may be called the heavenly alchemy, which changes iron into gold; by which is meant, that the most trivial and ordinary actions, when done to please God, become acts of divine love."

We must do all of our works of devotion (pious works, spiritual works) with the sole view of pleasing God rather than ourselves. This purity of intention is the basis for how much God will reward us for these actions. When we seek ourselves or praise from others for these actions, we lose all spiritual reward.

When we work to be pleasing to God, we are not vexed by whether the work appears to fail or succeed, whether it is noticed and praised by others or ignored and forgotten. We should not seek praise for our good works but nor should we avoid good works to avoid encountering praise. We must first act so as to please God and, second, act so as to give a good example to our neighbor.

When a pure intention accompanies all of our actions in a day, such that they are done in a manner, and with a desire, to please God, they become acts of divine love and make smooth our path to paradise.

~
Tepidity
~

"Souls that make no account of venial sins, and give themselves up to tepidity, without a thought of freeing themselves from it, live in great danger."

"Ven. Alvarez used to say, 'Those little backbitings, dislikes, culpable curiosity, acts of impatience and intemperance, do not indeed kill the soul, but they so weaken it, that when any great temptation takes it unexpectedly, it will not have strength enough to resist, and will consequently fall'."

"And let us rest assured that he who makes no progress in the way of God will always be going back; and he will go back so far that at last he will fall over some precipice."

Venial sins, committed with no concern for their remedy, place the sinner in great danger. These are not those committed out of human frailty, but those committed deliberately and habitually.

Souls who have received God's favor should fear that their deliberate venial sins, in which they let their love for God grow cold, have not only weakened their souls but that they have also deprived them of the divine assistance, for God is sparing to those who are sparing toward Him.[3]

Often this habit of deliberate sin is tied to a passionate attachment to some vice in which the person is bound and which is driving his behavior toward evil. This inordinate attachment can eventually inflame the passion toward more grievous, and more deadly, sins.

To eradicate an attachment to venial sin, in particular to that sin which is predominant in our soul, we must first desire to change that sinful habit. This good desire will lighten the burden and strengthen us to make progress in the way of God.

St. Alphonsus heavily emphasizes that we must take Jesus at His word, "Ask and you shall receive," and pray constantly. By this, we shall persevere and avoid sin.

~ Devotion to the Mother of God ~

A devotion to the Holy Mother of God, which is most efficacious and is taken up by those who wish to insure their eternal salvation, should fill one's day and accompany all of their prayers and acts.

St. Alphonsus says to make novenas ahead of the seven principal feasts of Our Lady. He does not list those dates but the following are some of the major Marian feast days: January 1 (Mother of God/Circumcision), February 2 (Purification of Our Lady/Candlemas), March 25 (The

---

[3] "Qui parce seminat, parce et metet." – 2 Cor. ix. 6.

Annunciation), May 31 (see footnote),[4] August 15 (The Assumption of Our Lady), August 22 (see footnote),[5] September 8 (The Nativity of Our Lady), December 8 (The Immaculate Conception).

~
Acquire the Love of Jesus Christ
~

To acquire the grace to love Jesus Christ, we must ask Him for this grace often, such as in our Communions and our visits to the Most Blessed Sacrament. We should also often ask for this grace from the hands of Our Lady, our guardian angel, and our patron saints.

"St. Francis de Sales says that the grace of loving Jesus Christ contains all other graces in itself; because he who truly loves Jesus Christ cannot be wanting in any virtue."

Our hearts must be detached from earthly affections in order to make sufficient room for divine love. The love and affection we have for creatures is love and affection that cannot be directed toward God.

When we pray, we should make acts of love to Jesus Christ, in which we state our love for Him, our joy from knowing that He is infinitely happy with the Father, and our desire that all men would know and love Him. These acts are the fuel by which we keep alive the love of God.

No spiritual exercise is more efficacious in kindling love for Jesus Christ than by meditating often on His Passion. While

---

[4] On this date, the Church traditionally celebrates the Queenship of Mary. In the modern calendar, the Church celebrates the Visitation of Our Lady. The Visitation is traditionally observed on July 2nd.

[5] On this date, the Church traditionally celebrates the Immaculate Heart of Mary. In the modern calendar, the Church celebrates the Queenship of Mary.

He could have saved us by a single prayer, He chose to do so by shedding every drop of His blood and, in doing this, to draw all hearts to Himself. When we meditate on His Passion, we do what is most agreeable to Him.

Slaying Dragons Press Classics

Slaying Dragons Press Classics is a new endeavor though one which has long been a desire of the Slaying Dragons Apostolate. In particular, there has been a desire to bring into print the marvelous and largely forgotten works of the master of morality and the spiritual life, St. Alphonsus Liguori.

With the desire to bring back into print many of his excellent writings, there has also been a felt need to make these writings intelligible to the modern Christian mind, often under-catechized and very much immersed in a materialistic and secular culture. Many Christians, even among the devout, have been deprived of the traditional teachings of the Church in the modern era. Great Christian writers such as St. Alphonsus Liguori are, therefore, greatly needed by the modern Church.

Slaying Dragons Press Classics intends to bring back many of his writings, presenting them in a way that preserves the integrity of the original and also presents some helpful analysis to assist the reader in remembering the key teachings.

This effort of bring back into print lost and marvelous writings of St. Alphonsus Liguori will not, God willing, be limited to this great Doctor of the Church alone. It is the hope that this effort will be able to present many more lost spiritual treasures to the faithful of today.

Slaying Dragons Press

Slaying Dragons Press, founded in 2021, is the fruit of a spiritual work begun in 2016 which sought to find new ways to bring people the joy and beauty of the Catholic Faith. By God's Providence, what began under the name *The Retreat Box* has grown into *The Slaying Dragons Apostolate* and *Slaying Dragons Press*.

This work is a grassroots apostolate which thrives on support and endorsements from those who enjoy these books. As a result, fans of the books and supporters of the mission help increase the reach of *Slaying Dragons Press* by telling friends, family, priests, religious, and Bishops about these books.

Please consider supporting this work in any way that you can. While *Slaying Dragons Press* is *not* a non-profit, financial support is always welcome. Please visit SlayingDragonsPress.com for ways to support this apostolate. If you do not have a copy of the other celebrated books we have published, get one today!

*Support this work on **Patreon**
~patreon.com/**theslayingdragonsapostolate**

*Subscribe to the author's website for discounts and news
~SlayingDragonsPress.com/pages/**Subscribe**

Popular *Slaying Dragons Press* Titles

The Occult Among Us: Exorcists and Former Occultists Expose the Nature of This Modern Evil

The Rise of the Occult: What Exorcists & Former Occultists Want You to Know

Slaying Dragons: What Exorcists See & What We Should Know (also in Spanish – *Matando Dragones*)

Slaying Dragons - Prepare for Battle: Applying the Wisdom of Exorcists to Your Spiritual Warfare

Swords and Shadows: Navigating Youth Amidst the Wiles of Satan

Come Away By Yourselves: A Guide to Prayer for Busy Catholics

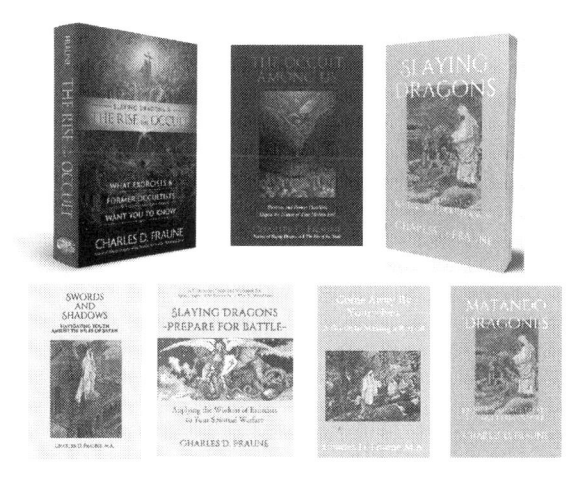

Slaying Dragons Press

Made in the USA
Columbia, SC
29 April 2025